HOPE AND HEALING
AFTER BREAST CANCER

JOURNEY TO

WHOLENESS

NANCY W. BROWN & SCOTT REALL

WITH SUSAN DAVENPORT, SARA HAMILL,
& MARCELLA TUDEEN

To find a Restore Small Group near you, please visit the following website: www.restoresmallgroups.org.

If you would like to invite Scott to speak to your church, community organization, or event, please visit www. restoresmallgroups.org

If you would like to donate to Restore Small Groups to help support the life-changing work of this ministry, please visit www.restoresmallgroups.org.

ISBN: 979-8-9889747-1-0

CONTENTS

RELATIONSHIP WITH OTHERS AND OURSELVES

MOVING THROUGH LIFE'S LOSSES

PROCESSING OUR LOSSES

ACCEPTANCE AND SEEING THE GIFTS

CREATING YOUR VISION PLAN

"I always get to where I'm going
by walking away from where I've been."
—WINNIE THE POOH

Change is an inevitable part of life. Sometimes we choose it, and sometimes change comes for us whether we want it or not. If you are here, it means your life has been changed in some way by a cancer diagnosis. For many, this has meant struggles with fear, uncertainty, loss, grief and a host of other emotions. For a few, it felt like a small speed bump in the road of life, when held up against other profound life challenges.

A cancer diagnosis is not simply an isolated event. Everything that makes you "you" influences your feelings and your reaction to your diagnosis. Your life experiences before cancer will help shape what life will look like going forward. But regardless of your situation, the fact remains that your life has been forever changed.

You now have an opportunity to stop and take a look at your life— both before and after cancer—and ask, "Is this the life I really want?"

During the next nine weeks, we will lean into community to contemplate this question.

Because we bring our entire lives to our diagnosis, we will examine areas that may have long been tucked away. We will also explore all our emotions, perhaps for the first time, and begin to really pay attention to how we feel. We will look at the losses throughout our lives, and in the safety of our small group, we'll process any lingering grief surrounding those losses (there will be some, whether you realize it now or not).

As women, most of us tend to innately seek out community—but cancer can be very isolating and change relationships in confusing ways. During our time together, we'll form bonds of a sisterhood like no other; many of these will last a lifetime. We'll nod with an understanding that's impossible for those who have not walked this path. We'll laugh. We'll cry. And we will emerge with a written plan that will be the basic blueprint to making the changes we want in order to have the life we desire.

We will travel on this journey together as we continually seek wholeness—emotionally, spiritually, and physically.

EXPLORING HOPE

*"There is no hope unmingled with fear,
no fear unmingled with hope."*

—BARUCH SPINOZA

"Truly it is in the darkness that one finds the light…"

—MEISTER ECKHART

*"The mystery of human existence lies not in just staying alive,
but in finding something to live for."*

—FYODOR DOSTOYEVSKY

HOPE VS WISHES

I was diagnosed with stage 3 breast cancer at the end of 2000. That makes it easy to do the math when I need to remember how long I've been a survivor. Wait, what? Do the math? That's right… sometimes I actually forget how many years it's been since my diagnosis.

Other memories feel as fresh as last night's TV show. Like how I clung to the hope it gave me when I met someone who was a double digit survivor, because every other minute was consumed by that monstrous fear that sat waiting like a wolf at the door… Every. Single. Day. I remember how my hope was a desperate wish that it was a mistake; the doctors were wrong and this wasn't really happening. Then my hope that God would miraculously take the cancer away if I prayed hard enough and my belief was strong enough. Those hope-wishes did not come true, so then my hope-wish was that I would survive the brutal treatment; that I would live to see my young children grow up.

Like you, I spent those first days numbly going to doctor appointments, trying to make decisions based on medical jargon that swept past me like cobwebs in the dark. I cried. A lot. I got really, really angry and yelled at God at the top of my lungs.

But then one day something happened. I was doing laundry, trying to keep some sense of routine and normalcy while my world was in chaos. A huge thought smacked me right between the eyes. I very suddenly realized that I had a choice.

I could choose to mope around, crying and angry, feeling sorry for myself. Or, I could choose to accept what had happened and make the most of whatever time I had left... whether that was one year or fifty. At that moment, I decided that cancer would not win. My prayer changed from "take this away" to "let this have some meaning."

And that, my fellow survivors, is hope.

The definition of hope is believing in the possibility that things will get better, not just physically but emotionally, mentally and spiritually too. Real hope is not the same as a wish. True hope requires our commitment. A wish is tied to outcomes like wishing that our cancer won't come back. If my hope is tied to only one outcome, then my hope is wishing. There is a difference between desire (wishes) and hope. I can wish for the disease to go away and never come back, which is normal, but true hope is not tied to that, or any, circumstance.

Wishes are superficial and usually self-serving. Imagine blowing out birthday candles as a child. The wishes you made related to something you wanted for yourself. Hope requires faith and is deeper level— almost like a verb. It is active.

True hope is the faith that God will take bad things and make good come out of it, while still accepting that we cannot and do not understand why bad things have to happen at all. Hope leaves the outcome to God. Henri Nouwen writes, "Hope is trusting that something will be fulfilled, but fulfilled according to the promises and not just according to our wishes. Therefore, hope is always open ended," leaving the outcome to God.[1]

One group participant shared that she loved the term "open-ended hope" for several reasons. She said, "I know what I hope but because I have faith I'm leaving the outcome to God. We don't have to have a conclusion in open-ended hope."

What that means is that open-ended hope believes in spite of circumstances. It is having faith that God wants the best for us, even if we don't understand the circumstances we're in, and that we will be taken care of. This is true hope, and it does not come easily. For most of us, it is a process of taking daily small steps; intentionally looking to the Spirit within to calm our fears and strengthen our trust.

It's a fact that the idea of hope has been studied repeatedly through the years. Hope breeds more hope and studies have shown that those who have higher levels of hope show better adaptation to life's curveballs. Having true hope is also associated with lower stress levels, less anxiety and depression and being able to feel more involved in the "pace" of your own life.

Hope is a fundamental part of change and the ability to move forward in life. It was a turning point for me when I realized that even though I couldn't change my circumstance, I could change my response. That realization didn't mean I never had days of doubt, fear or anger ever again. But changing my response was the first small step toward hope, followed by many others. The goal of every day is to trust at all times that God is with you and will meet your needs. Finding hope is a matter of trust.

REFLECTIONS

1. What does open-ended hope mean to you?

2. How do you find true hope in times of darkness and uncertainty?

3. How does hope influence my outlook on life and my future?

BITTER VS BETTER

Once treatment ends and life is back to "normal," we often look back and see our diagnosis as a line in the sand; life is now very clearly divided into "BC" and "AC." Whatever life was like Before Cancer, it feels different After Cancer. We have been transported, willingly or not, into a new life.

We frequently hear this called our "new normal." We may have liked our old normal just fine. But one of the gifts of this diagnosis is that it often makes us take time-out to evaluate our true worth and our authentic vision for our lives. By looking for our best life, we can turn this "crisis" into a positive. The author C.S. Lewis says that pain is "God's megaphone" and its pain forces us to search inward.[2] The choice is ours—will we choose to be bitter or better?

We have all heard that it is darkest before the dawn. We become overwhelmed, and fall to our knees and ask for help. Breast cancer survivor Leigh shared that it was in this "darkness" that she found her beginning. She leaned on Psalms 139:12 (NIV) for her strength. "Even the darkness will not be dark to you. The night will shine like the day for darkness is as light to you." To Leigh this meant even her dark days were not dark to God because he saw the light moments that were coming after, just like the dawn emerges each morning from the night.

Even though we may desperately want to get back to our old normal, most of us find that not only has the definition of normal drastically changed, but "normal" is actually nowhere to be found. It's now part of our past. We may not be able to do the things we once did, or maybe doing those things takes us longer. Our joints may feel old and stiff. Relationships may have shifted. On the other hand, we no longer sweat the small stuff; priorities are now in sharp focus. There is often a desire to waste less time. Maybe for you that means doing more or pursuing a dream. For others, that may mean doing less and learning how to just "be" instead of "do."

Open-ended hope is receptive to change. It is not dedicated to doing the same things over and over again with the same old results. Hope thinks new thoughts. A young survivor once emphatically stated to me how much she disliked the term "new normal." She said that she felt instead like an updated, improved version of herself in spite of the new aches and pains.

Although she had been happy with her life "BC" as a wife and mother with a career she enjoyed, after cancer she confronted her fear of living a different way. She opened her mind to a new kind of life. She opened her mind to hope. The goal every day is to make life better, not perfect and not exactly as it was.

Inevitably life will bring more obstacles. But open-ended hope carries us through. Consider and reconsider what brings you hope. Nurture that. Hope and acceptance are two sides of the same coin. By accepting things we can't change, we give up trying to control our circumstances. Yet it also allows us to focus on what we can change and move toward the full potential of our life. There will be ups and downs for every single one of us—breast cancer or no breast cancer. But open-ended hope carries us through. We can embrace this joy in "AC." The Serenity Prayer is a great place to start when beginning a vision for new life going forward.

SERENITY PRAYER

*God grant me the serenity to accept
the things I cannot change, Courage
to change the things I can,
And wisdom to know the difference.*

—REINHOLD NIEBUHR,
ADAPTED BY WINNIFRED CRANE WYGALX

REFLECTIONS

1. What "small stuff" did you used to sweat that you've now let go?

2. Are there old normals that you don't want to return to? If so, what?

3. Tell about a time where you have experienced light after darkness?

DO YOU WANT TO BE MADE WELL?

When we talk about making life changes after a cancer diagnosis, many women think of lifestyle changes like diet, exercise, and stress reduction. While those are all worthwhile changes, sometimes the areas of our lives in need of change are much more subtle and difficult to recognize. You are here because of a health crisis, but what was going on in your life before your diagnosis? How were your relationships working? Did you feel a sense of purpose? Did you struggle with unresolved problems or regret? Have you experienced loss before? Are you where you wanted to be in life? Perhaps you felt at a dead end, confused and just knew something needed to change. This is all okay. This contemplation of change is the spadework, but change can't happen unless we first believe in the possibility of it.

There is a story about Pope Julius II watching Michelangelo hammering away at a slab of marble. "Why are you working so hard?" he asked. Michelangelo replied, "Can't you see there's an angel imprisoned in this block of stone? I'm working as hard as I can to set her free."[3] Inside us is the person we were meant to be. We may have lost that person after years of hurt, disappointment or just taking care of others and putting our own needs last. We only need to chip away the parts that hold us captive to fear, low self-esteem, to feeling unworthy to be loved by God and others. Change is what happens when we break free from these hindrances.

We have to believe in the possibility of change before we can be set free. We also need to ask some tough questions about the life we have and the life we want. We can't do this alone. We need the help of others, especially those on a similar journey. Holding in our emotions and needs is like holding a balloon under water. It will eventually rush to the surface. In a healing community, we have a safe space to let go of anything that is holding us back, and that balloon **can** take you soaring to new heights… **if** you let it.

But just like most things in life, nothing much happens without concrete action steps. You may not know how to take the first step right now, and that's okay. It's a process we'll explore together in the coming weeks. At this moment, the only step you need to take is to consider if you're willing to envision a new future.

The Bible has a story about a paralyzed man lying near the Pool of Bethesda.[4] The waters of the pool were said to heal, but the man could not physically lift himself into the pool. Every day, he wished for a chance to be healed. He encounters Jesus at the pool who asks the question: "Do you want to be made well?" Jesus did not doubt the man's sincerity in wanting healing. He'd been lying by the pool for 38 years. The paralyzed man thought that he wanted to be made well, but Jesus was asking something different. In essence he was saying, "A healing will change you forever. You will have to learn a completely new way of life." Jesus was not questioning whether healing is good, only whether the man understood what he was asking for; what he would have to do to enjoy his new freedom.

The power in this process of change is in the specifics: we must name what we want to be different, and we must own it. Think of your life thus far as a slab of marble and look inside for the angel. What do you see? Who, and what is truly important? As you begin to formulate answers, you will start to see your angel in the stone more clearly.

Many women say they feel unsettled. Often there is a call to do something that feels more meaningful. Suzie is a physician, and after treatment ended she thought she might go to Africa and work in a refugee camp. This experience brings change, and frequently, it also stirs in us a desire to make additional changes—to chip away the stone and find our authentic selves.

The underlying message is you'll have to learn a new way of life. Take concrete steps and be willing to do the work. **You** have a part in your own healing.

REFLECTIONS

1. If Jesus was standing in front of you asking if you want to be "made well," what would you say to him?

2. What does "being made well" mean to you?

3. What are some concrete steps you would have to take to make this happen?

FACING OUR INNER CRITIC

We may doubt that we can become the person we envision. The grief of our cancer diagnosis may also intertwine with the grief and regret that we have about other parts of our lives. Past mistakes, failures, hurts, and disappointments, from childhood onward, provide fuel for experiencing repeating negative thoughts. These thoughts may hold us back from true self-compassion and keep us stuck. We often refer to these negative thoughts as the "inner critic," the voice that reminds us of our inadequacies and leaves us feeling unworthy and unlovable.

The inner critic can show up at any time in our life and usually has its origin in the other people who have, in spoken or unspoken ways, given us negative feedback over our lifetime.

Perhaps you can relate to making a mistake and telling yourself, "How could I have been so stupid?" or looking in the mirror and thinking "I'm so ugly. I wish I could change…" The inner critic is unforgiving.

It uses comparison to devalue. It compares us to those who seemingly have the things we desire, whether that's beauty, health, prestige or power. Never does it compare us to those who have less. It makes us feel as if we are the only ones deprived of the "good life." This causes us to feel devalued, as if we are second-class citizens. It whispers messages to us about all the things we "should" do or the person we "should" be, not necessarily the things we can do for our health, peace and well-being.

As we are forced to slow down and focus on our life, we may hear many different voices talking to us. They may tell us that we didn't take care of ourselves enough and so we are now suffering the consequences. Or that we have not done enough with our lives. We may start to feel the sting of relationship troubles. We may feel that we're a burden to others, unlovable, unattractive, isolated. We may question our purpose.

But we must not let the inner critic win. Giving the microphone to that negative inner voice is just bullying ourselves and no one likes a bully. So why do we allow this to happen? Try thinking about yourself as the real prize that you are. Think of the cheering you so graciously offer up to others. By disputing our inner critic we will silence it. It's time to start cheering inwardly and give ourselves the grace we deserve. There is a purpose for our cancer experience, and we can transform this pain over time into something new. We may find that others tell us now more than ever that we are courageous, but we may not feel even remotely this way. After all, we're simply doing what we have to in the face of our diagnosis. In many ways, it's like being placed on the front line of the battlefield and because we are standing there, we are now considered heroes. But we never wanted to be there in the first place.

Once in a Journey To Wholeness (JTW) small group, a facilitator asked the women in her group to write the number one thing that their inner critic whispers to them. Once everyone had written their responses, she asked them to turn to the person on their right and say it to them as if they were the targets of those words. Everyone gasped and of course said, "No, I could never say that to her!" When asked by the facilitator why they couldn't share—one participant said it was because she didn't want to hurt others feelings. Another woman said, "Because it's probably not true." This is an aha moment. We wouldn't say these negative things to others, yet we tell them to ourselves. Even if it hurts our own feelings and probably isn't true of us either.

We may not immediately know the purpose of the pain and suffering in our life. It may simply be to provide an example of courage to someone else who is struggling. Perhaps it is the catalyst for change in our life that will ultimately change the world; or maybe just our little corner of it. My inner critic held me captive for many years, but the character I found within myself as I went through my cancer diagnosis, treatment, and recovery prepared me for my role to help other women with cancer. I believe God led me to help others. Without this experience, I may never have found my passion and purpose.

If we remember that we are "fearfully and wonderfully made"[5] in God's image, we can be confident that our individual talents, skills, characteristics, strengths and even weaknesses are part of a greater purpose that God designed in ultimate wisdom. When your inner critic whispers negative messages, try counteracting it with something positive. Every time you start to feel badly about yourself, think about an accomplishment. Maybe you couldn't clean the entire house, but you got the laundry done. Don't discount the positive. Change takes place when we learn not to listen to the inner critic but instead listen to God. You are special because God created the unique you!

REFLECTIONS

1. What does your inner critic say to you most often? Write one truth about yourself that counters that negative voice.

2. Are you experiencing any negative messages around your diagnosis? (Example: self-blame, survivors guilt, etc)

3. Share one of your early memories of experiencing a negative message.

DOING THE CHA-CHA

The majority of the survivors that I have worked with over the years list weight loss as one of their goals. The same majority also say they've tried to lose weight and have failed. This may be an ongoing pattern of behavior or it may be a new experience, but it almost always results in the negative thought, "I can't lose weight so why should I even keep trying?"

Weight gain is one of the almost inevitable side effects of breast cancer treatment and can really give fuel to our inner critic. Although some weight gain is a physiologic response to medications and lack of estrogen, there is still much that can be done to minimize this unwelcome situation. It may require some lifestyle changes, though, so we must truly desire to lose the weight.

Lewis Smedes says that this is the first thing going on inside us when we hope for something: we must desire what we hope for enough that we are willing to make whatever changes are necessary to achieve it.[6] This is what distinguishes hope from a wish. Hope is a verb; it is active. A wish is passive; it's all talk and no action.

One important concept for this new journey is learning to "train" and not just to "try." Willpower is an element of change, but it is not the deciding factor. Training versus trying is the key to success. When we try to change and do not succeed, we tend to give up after a few attempts. But when we train to do something, we set our minds on learning. No matter how many times we fail, we see ourselves as being one step closer to succeeding. Trying is the raw use of willpower, nothing more. Training is learning the life skills needed for a long-term change.

Think about Olympic athletes. They don't just show up one day and try to win a gold medal, they spend years envisioning success and training their bodies to perform at their peak.

The key in the process of lasting change is to balance the spirit, mind and body. Even though we might be a physical specimen of robust health, our spirit may be malnourished and before long, there is a disconnection.

As Gerald May wrote, "Both Eastern and Western medical sciences have long understood that maintaining natural balances is the body's greatest priority; if the systems of the body are going to work at all, they must work together in harmony."[7]

The key here is to give ourselves time. The goal is progress, not perfection. Expect setbacks. That is how we learn and grow. Change doesn't happen with one large leap, but with multiple baby steps. One survivor shared her goal after her double mastectomy was to return to her previously active lifestyle. Not accustomed to sitting still for long periods of time—it was difficult for her to rest. When the time came for her to start regaining her stamina—she found that she had to ease her way back in. Her first walk consisted of going two houses down and back. The next day she added one more house to her plan, and so on and so on. Some days she was too tired to keep her normal pace and route. Baby steps. Robert Brault once said an optimist is "someone who figures that taking a step backward after taking a step forward is not a disaster, it's a cha-cha."[8] James Prochaska echoes the same in his many years of research around personal change. Instead of using the word "relapse" for those who have a setback, he prefers the word "recycling." He says, "several such setbacks may make you feel as though you are going around in circles rather than solving your problem. And to some extent, that is the case, but the good news is that the circles are spiraling upward...recycling gives us opportunities to learn."[9]

The most lasting change comes when we are intrinsically motivated. Being intrinsically motivated means we have an internal desire to be different, to focus on who we want to be. We commit to being in it for the long haul not because we have to, but because we want to. We are not deciding to change simply because someone else desires it for us or because we are scared of the external consequences of not changing. We give ourselves the time, the grace and the permission to work through our mistakes.

Extrinsic motivation, on the other hand, is the fear of external consequences. An example of the difference between the two: I may be extrinsically motivated to clean up my diet and begin an exercise program because the doctor says if I don't, I may develop diabetes and that scares me. Being intrinsically motivated to alter my diet happens because it is important to take care of myself. I want to make the most of my life and enjoy my time with my family and loved ones. Although the desire to get healthier may initially come from extrinsic motivation—we will only maintain these changes over time if we have a sincere desire to be healthy because we believe we are worthy of good health. Extrinsic motivation comes from outside us, from not wanting a certain consequence. It will not sustain a new habit or lifestyle because eventually the fear will subside and the motivation disappears.

So, the challenge as we slowly process this new normality is to allow ourselves to grieve the loss of our old lives, contemplate what changes we need to embrace or make, and then give ourselves time to train, find balance and locate our true motivation.

REFLECTIONS

1. Have you grieved the loss of your old life? Please explain.

2. What do you want to tell the "you" before cancer?

3. List some baby steps you can take now to train toward living balanced in body, mind and spirit.

PURPOSE FUELS HOPE

During World War II, the Nazis set up a camp where prisoners worked, surrounded by barbaric conditions. One day, the prisoners were ordered to move a huge pile of garbage from one end of the camp to another. The next day, they were ordered to move the pile back to its original location. No reason was given, they were just told to do it. So began a pattern: day after day, the prisoners hauled the same mountain of garbage from one end of the camp to the other.

The impact on the prisoners of that mindless, meaningless labor and existence began to come to the surface. An elderly prisoner began sobbing uncontrollably and had to be led away. Then another man began screaming until he was beaten into silence. A third man suddenly broke away and began running toward the electric fence. He was told to stop or he'd be electrocuted. He didn't care. He flung himself on the fence and died in a blinding flash.

In the days that followed, dozens of prisoners became despondent. Their captors didn't care, for what the prisoners didn't know was that they were part of an experiment in mental health. The Nazis wanted to determine what would happen when people were subjected to meaningless activity. They wanted to see what a life would become without a sense of purpose.

Meaning is decisive to human existence. We all need a purpose. We need to know that our lives matter. This is why the Bible encourages us that God, has "good plans for you, not plans to hurt you. Plans to give you hope and a good future." (Jeremiah 29:11) Hope is important to our future, and the great thing about hope is that God gives it freely.

Many of us ride the currents of our lives without much thought about the direction in which we're headed. For some, life is a big comfy float drifting around a lazy river in dappled sunshine and warm breezes with a cold drink in hand. Others find themselves in a whitewater raft, dodging sharp boulders in the rush toward a tumbling waterfall. Wherever we fall on this spectrum—it's safe to say that we want the reward and not the struggle. The results and not the process. But life doesn't happen TO us, it happens FOR us.

Whatever life was like before, a cancer diagnosis is a harsh interruption. Life as we knew it falls apart, and we seek to put it back together with a greater sense of purpose in mind. While we may find purpose in being a partner, a mother, in our jobs, or in leisure pursuits, there may now be a restlessness; a yearning for more.

In my experience, women unanimously agree that they want their cancer experience to have some meaning. It seems as if that makes everything we've been through worthwhile. We want to know God's purpose for our lives. As we strive for confident hope, we realize that we are happier focusing on how we will live, not on how long.

One survivor recalled being in bed sick for her high schooler's first day of school his senior year. As she watched all the Facebook posts of everyone's "First Day Of School" pictures she felt a wave of sadness. She had nothing to contribute for this milestone day. She felt useless and shared that she felt like she was being a burden to her family on a day that should be celebratory. She was too sick to even care for her own family and wanted to feel productive and meaningful. She was too sick to go to work which added to her feelings of uselessness. When she shared her sentiments with her brother he said, "Actually, you DO have a job right now. Your job is fighting for your life. Go to the doctor. Take the meds. Get the chemo. Have the surgeries. Take naps! Those things are your job right now and we all need you to do your job." That totally changed her perspective and she then realized those who loved her—needed her to do *that* job.

Viktor Frankel writes: "We must never forget that we may also find meaning in life even when confronted with a hopeless situation, when facing a fate that cannot be changed. For what then matters is to bear witness to the uniquely human potential at its best, which is to transform a personal tragedy into a triumph, to turn one's predicament into a human achievement. When we are no longer able to change a situation… we are challenged to change ourselves. In some way, suffering ceases to be suffering at the moment it finds a meaning."[10]

This moment in time is an opportunity to refocus our lives and to clear away those things that are distractions from our true purpose and joy. What are those things for you? What is wasting your time?

REFLECTIONS

1. What makes you feel significant and purposeful?

2. Share how you can see that your suffering could possibly be contributing to the meaning of your life.

3. What would others say you have to offer?

POWERLESSNESS:
AN ANSWER TO FEAR

"Sometimes you don't realize your own strength until you come face to face with your greatest weakness."
—SUSAN GALE

"You gain strength, courage and confidence by every experience in which you really stop to look fear in the face."
—ELEANOR ROOSEVELT

"You cannot heal what you do not first acknowledge."
—RICHARD ROHR

NAMING OUR FEARS

There is no escaping the fact that we are forever changed by our diagnosis. It is impossible to come face to face with one's own mortality and not look at life differently. We now understand in a whole new way that we are not in control. The fear can be paralyzing. These are no trivial realities.

The women that I've met with breast cancer throughout the years show remarkable resiliency, the ability to bounce back after a tragic or traumatic event. Breast cancer is both tragic and traumatic, but we just put one foot in front of the other and do what we must to get through it. We live each day to the fullest and look for the gifts in the midst of all the chaos and uncertainty.

At diagnosis we are overwhelmed, full of fear, perhaps angry. We may question God. But in the busyness of months of treatment, we shove these feelings to the background and simply look for the light at the end of the tunnel. We probably don't realize it at the time, but we get comfortable with seeing our care team of physicians, nurses, and technicians every few weeks.

We may hate the treatments themselves, but put a certain amount of trust into believing they are getting rid of the cancer. Our anxiety subsides a bit.

We look forward to the end of treatment, counting the days until we can get "back to normal." Then it happens—one day we ring the bell, get our certificate of completion, and the doctor says, "See you in three months." Before long, it's "see you in six months." Without the rhythm and routine of regular visits, fear makes an unexpected return. I like to say it feels like walking a tightrope without a safety net.

Most survivors are surprised to find themselves once again gripped by fear when treatment is over. The seemingly sudden onslaught of emotions takes us off guard. It's like a dam breaking. Once we have time to stop and think about what has just happened, all the emotions and doubts we didn't have time for come rushing to the surface. "All these months I've been waiting to get back to normal, but everything is different now. I can't go back to the way I was," is the collective observation.

One of the ways we can overcome this new wave of fear is to name it—what is it, specifically, that we are afraid of ? "Recurrence" is such a broad, vague catch-all. Are you afraid of death? Are you afraid of leaving loved ones? Do you fear pain? There is often fear surrounding physical changes—what will my body look like? Will my partner find me attractive and lovable? Will I be able to physically do everything I did before?

We once again become profoundly aware of our own mortality as the "what ifs" seem to slam into our thoughts with more intensity. When these "what ifs" are coming fast and furious, we have a choice. We can choose to trust God, or we can be paralyzed by fear. This goes back to the first week when we talked about the real meaning of hope.

The elephant in the room is what we all know and are afraid to say out loud: we are all going to die someday. Charles Franklin said, "No one gets out of this life alive. So leave a footprint of your choice. You are writing your epitaph. You are writing it now! Life is a process, not a goal. Live it now, or you will miss it! We have time to spend and no time to waste."[11] It sounds cliché to say that we might get run over by a truck this afternoon, but it's true.

The gift of our diagnosis is that we are now fully aware of our mortality, which gives us an urgency to live life to the fullest. We want to be more alive in the truest sense of the word: not physically, but emotionally. The emphasis is now on quality rather than quantity—since nobody knows how much time they will have on earth, the focus is on making the time we have the best it can be.

REFLECTIONS

1. How does fear or anxiety impact your day to day life?

2. What specific fears are you experiencing? List your fears.

3. When you experience fear or anxiety, what is something you can do to help let go of it? How can you feel more peace?

MAKING PEACE WITH FEAR

Perhaps of more consequence than the fear of recurrence, or even the fear of dying, are the fears that are a part of the human condition; those deeply hidden fears that we try to ignore and certainly don't admit.

Fear can take place in many areas of life. In fact, our brains are wired to register potential negative outcomes as a means of survival. Psychotherapist and author Thom Rutledge writes, "Fear is our constant companion, our day-to-day nemesis, and our ultimate challenge. Fear fuels our negative and judgmental thoughts and our need to control things."[12]

Irvin Yalom identified the four key fears[13] with which we struggle:

Fear of death
Fear of freedom
Fear of isolation, and
Fear of meaninglessness

Almost all of us wrestle with these fears at one time or another. Out of the four, the fears of isolation and meaninglessness may be the most difficult to bear.

Another fear almost everyone shares is a deep conviction of basic inadequacy, a feeling of being incompetent in everything we do. We may think we are not smart enough, pretty enough, or skilled enough. In essence, we are saying, "If you really knew me, you would reject me." As we discussed in Day 4, these fears come from someone or someplace in our life experience. If we have taken risks in life and have been emotionally, physically, or spiritually wounded, it is very hard to want to risk again. We want to be absolutely certain that no one will reject us before we take any kind of risk, whether that's speaking in public or opening up to an intimate relationship. We want to be guaranteed that if we take a risk, we will not experience humiliation, failure or rejection.

This is impossible, of course, and so many of us go through life avoiding risks which block us from striving for new things or reaching our full potential. It can become a very controlling, crippling influence. We avoid the things we fear, but we are also avoiding our chances to grow.

All through the Bible, God directly speaks to us about fear. Over and over God reminds us, "Be strong and of good courage; do not be afraid!" (Joshua 1:9 NKJV) Even if we're walking through "the valley of the shadow of death," we are told not to be afraid because God is with us. (Psalm 23) So, how do we begin to feel secure enough to risk? The psalmist also says, "I said, 'I am about to fall,' but, Lord, your love kept me safe." (Psalm 94:18) The antidote to our fears is to form secure attachments, to God and to others. Secure attachments help us diminish fear. If we do not have a safe place and safe people to be our authentic selves and to be accepted for who we truly are, we will always be reluctant to risk for fear of being hurt or isolated. We need to build our support system and slowly learn to trust others and God with our lives because secure attachments are vital to our emotional healing. As the saying goes, we can create our "family of choice," surrounding ourselves with a life that honors who we are.

The early Native Americans had a unique practice of training young braves. On the night of their 13th birthday, after learning how to hunt, scout, and fish, he was put to one final test. He was placed in a dense forest to spend the entire night alone. Until then, he had never been away from the security of his family and the tribe. But on this night, he was blindfolded and taken several miles away. When he took the blindfold off, he was in the middle of the thick woods and he was terrified. Each time a twig snapped he imagined a wild animal ready to pounce. After what seemed like an eternity, dawn broke and the first rays of sunlight entered the interior of the forest. Looking around the boy saw flowers, trees, and the outline of the path. Then to his utter astonishment, he beheld the figure of a man standing just a few feet away, armed with a bow and arrow. It was his father. He had been there all night.

Being on the journey to wholeness means we trust at all times that God is with us and will meet our needs. His love is all-around. Even when we can't see or feel Him—He is here!

It takes a vision, intention, and purpose to defeat fear. Fear gains its strength from our retreat and it diminishes as we step into it. As author Susan Jeffers writes in her book, *Feel the Fear and Do It Anyway*, "We cannot escape fear. We can only transform it into a companion that accompanies us on our exciting adventures...Take a risk today—one small or bold stroke that will make you feel great once you have done it."[14] We can start with a small step and see how it goes. If we have trouble trusting, we can relearn this trust a little at a time.

Use this acronym to help you remember:

F – face it

E – explore it

A – accept it

R – develop a new response to it.

REFLECTIONS

1. Is there a risk(s) you want to take but are afraid to?

2. Who are your secure attachments—the people who know the true, authentic you?

3. Which of the four core fears listed is your greatest fear and why?

LETTING GO OF CONTROL

We live in a society that expects and rewards being in control. How many times have you heard someone say they're a "control freak?" Maybe you've said it yourself. As parents, we are compelled to control certain things with our children and families, just to limit the chaos and keep the family running. At work, we're expected to take charge of our area of responsibility. We are told to control our finances, our health, our appearance, our achievements, our future. We're used to making plans and having life happen according to those plans.

But the moment we find a lump or get called back because of a "suspicious" mammogram, we are forced to give up this common illusion of having control of our life. Suddenly, every day is filled with doctor's appointments, tests, chemo, radiation, surgery, doctor appointments and more doctor appointments. Everything revolves around treatment. We lose control of our bodies, our time, our normal routines.

We face the reality that is true for everyone: we never were in control, really. It's just that now that truth is no longer abstract, it is tangible. We are acutely aware that we have no control over this disease. We may have done everything right, and we still can't control the outcome. It's quite natural to feel more than a little fear when confronted by this reality, but if we are struggling with fear, we are struggling with control.

We want control over our circumstances; we even want to control God so that we get the outcome we desire. But that's not the way it works.

We can't change our circumstances, but God uses our circumstances to change us.

I realized that I could not change my circumstance and focused on my response instead. When we open our thoughts to embrace a new, unexpected version of our lives, those are small moments of trust where we acknowledge that God is in control. If open-ended hope is a matter of trust, then to have true hope we must hand the reins over to a power greater than ourselves. We trust God to take care of our needs each day because that's what is promised; nothing can separate us from God's love.[15] Developing this type of confident hope is a process, but when we have a small victory it brings an incredible sense of freedom. When we "let go and let God" take control, we no longer have to bear the burden.

Though we cannot ultimately control the outcome of the cancer journey, we can control our response and set goals to become healthier people. Theologian Lewes Smedes says that "hope builds on possibilities."[16] He explains that we simply start with one small step of faith. Set one small goal. Give yourself the grace of time, taking baby steps to achieve one goal at a time. Baby steps help us build momentum. They reduce the overwhelm. Each goal accomplished brings hope that others will also be reached.

After weeks or months of treatment and limited activity, starting an appropriate exercise program can be a healthy response to our experience. I met cancer survivor, Sharon, when she was in her mid-sixties, after devoting most of her adult life to raising children and working to help pay the bills. "It was just a job and I always resented a little because it kept me pretty sedentary. After chemo, I wasn't sure I'd ever have the energy to play with my grandkids or do all the other things I wanted to do. I was hopeful, but feeling a little defeated, too."

Sharon was a little hesitant the first time she was encouraged by her trainer to lift heavier weights during her workouts, but became much more confident when she found that it wasn't as hard as she expected. One day she reported having to buy new workout pants because the originals were too big. That encouraged her to limit her nightly ice cream to Fridays only. In a few more weeks she shared that she sent her husband out of town for the weekend and mulched the garden by herself, just because she wanted to! Over the course of several weeks, I saw Sharon emerge from a quiet, somewhat shy woman to a strong, confident, outgoing personality who delighted in encouraging others to go for their dreams. She told me, "When I stopped trying to eat the whole elephant in one bite and focused on one little baby step at a time, I was able to celebrate each small success. Feeling my body get stronger and stronger gave me the confidence to realize I could do other things, too. I didn't feel defeated anymore because I knew I had it in me to work toward all my other goals. I didn't need to lay them aside after all."

REFLECTIONS

1. Name the things you truly have control over.

2. What are you still trying to control that is actually out of your control?

3. When you feel life is out of control, how do you cope? Is this a healthy or unhealthy response?

CHANGING OUR PARADIGM

We bring our entire lives to our cancer diagnosis. It is not an isolated event. All the happy times and bad things that have occurred, the people we have known, the relationships we've had, the places we've been, the memories we've made, the successes and the failures, the mistakes and the times we got it right… all these things blend together into our human condition. Our experiences make us all unique individuals, and it will direct our response to any given situation.

Our life story creates our paradigm. A paradigm is our inner narrative, our unique perspective, that prompts us to respond to life's circumstances based on past experiences. One of the greatest things we can learn is to step back from our paradigm and realize it is only one "lens" through which to see the world. Others may see the world in a different way than we do. By sharing our narratives, we can expand, challenge and change our paradigm; when we shift and broaden our paradigm we are able to choose a different response.

Another way to explain our paradigm is to think of it as one window in a house. What we can see through the one window is limited. How we describe what we see outside the window is shaped by who we are and what we choose to focus on. But there are other windows in the house to look through that hold another perspective. There is no need to feel badly about our perspective, our "window." We can't change the experiences that have shaped our paradigm, but we can begin to process our experience in a different way. Views are different from every window of the house just like the perspective of everyone in our group is different. Being in community helps us see a different view.

It's impossible to do this in isolation. We need to process our thoughts and emotions with others we trust. We need to say it out loud. It's hard to do because we are wired to protect ourselves. But when we do, we gain clarity and perspective on our story. We open ourselves up to receiving compassion and mercy for the things we have been through and realize that we are not alone. A small group, especially one whose members share a similar life circumstance, can often provide that safe space to be vulnerable.

We may feel that in order to survive life, we have to be self-sufficient and independent, in control and driving our destiny. By shifting our paradigm of self-sufficiency to one of dependency on a power greater than ourselves and others to help, we work toward finding freedom from the fear of things we cannot control. We learn to trust the One who made us, loves us, and promises to keep us safe and never harm us.

In the book of Matthew in the Bible, there is a story called the "Sermon on Mount."[17] In this story, Jesus speaks to the crowd with a series of eight statements about different life circumstances. Known as the Beatitudes, the first one says, "Blessed are the poor in spirit, for theirs is the kingdom of heaven." In this statement, Jesus is explaining the importance of our dependence on God and others instead of ourselves, especially in times of difficulty. It is a statement on the importance of humility. For many, if not most, of us, there will be something along the way that breaks us and brings us to our knees. We come to the end of ourselves, the end of control. We realize that we are finite and limited. This is powerlessness. This is actually the most blessed place to be because we look God in the face and stop trying to control our own lives.

What Jesus was saying in this Beatitude is that when we are broken, God will give us strength. Powerlessness is not the same as helplessness. Helplessness means that we are victims of our circumstances, and that we have no hope of change. Powerlessness is admitting that we cannot control anything outside of ourselves, our actions and our responses. There is open-ended hope in powerlessness.

It seems that every day, we still try to "manage" those things that remain outside our control. There is tremendous emotional and spiritual freedom in laying down the heavy burden of all that control and giving it over to our Creator. But it is not easy. Powerlessness is a spiritual way of life that we must practice daily. Each day, try finishing this sentence for anything that applies, "I am powerless over my need to manage....." Whatever those places are, name them and let go of them. This journey to wholeness is an opportunity to let God and others share the load with us and to surrender our fears.

REFLECTIONS

1. What does powerlessness mean to you?

2. What were you powerless over during your cancer journey?

3. How can powerlessness be a gift?

THE GIFT OF FEELINGS

Our emotional lives are not only constantly active, they are also very complex. Throughout a day, our feelings are very often triggered, meaning they become very noticeable through situations, processes or actions that remind us of previous experiences.

Sometimes we know what is happening to us during these moments, and other times we can be very surprised by the level of emotional reaction we have to people, places and situations. Fear is a primary emotion for us during this experience, but we will also feel an entire world of fluctuating emotions. It is important to grow awareness around our emotional lives and become more mindful of our feelings and how we're going to process them.

The anniversary of our diagnosis or surgery can be a powerful trigger, as can returning for checkups, mammograms or other procedures. We may experience dread, fear, anger, hurt, sadness, or even shame or guilt.

Spring is a trigger for me. Every year as the weather gets warm, the trees start to bloom and the sky is that bright blue unique to the season, I walk in my neighborhood and feel both incredible sadness and immense joy all at the same time. I was in the middle of chemo during spring, and an acquaintance from church was also in treatment for a different type of cancer. He was always quick with a word of encouragement, a prayer, or a flower from his yard. We talked about how the red of the cardinals stood out so vividly against the blue of the sky. And then one day he was gone. He went to bed one night and didn't wake up. To this day I think of him every time I see a bright red cardinal against a vividly blue spring sky and feel the stabbing sadness of his loss. But because I can anticipate and recognize the sadness, I allow myself to feel it fully and honor the person that I lost.

Some of the women that I have worked with over the years feel guilty because their diagnosis and treatment wasn't "as bad" as someone else they knew, or because they're in remission and someone else is not. This is so common it actually has a name: survivor guilt. We may wonder why—what did we do, or what didn't we do, differently from them? The truth is, we have no control over this.

The side effects of treatment and ongoing maintenance medications, especially hormone inhibitors, can be daily reminders that we are no longer the person we once were. This can trigger many emotions: hurt, anger, loneliness, shame... We realize we have no control over what we're experiencing and struggle to find acceptance and make the best of it. What we need to understand is that these feelings are natural, and that they are neither good nor bad—they just are. What is important is how we choose to respond to these feelings. But first, we need to acknowledge that these feelings exist; we need to feel our feelings.

Through diagnosis and treatment and into survivorship, we have probably had days when we experienced so many feelings we could not distinguish one from the other. And there have probably been days when we could not bear to feel anything and simply shut down. Dr. Chip Dodd says, "Feelings are the voice of the heart. And you will not have fullness unless you are adept at hearing and experiencing all of them. When you are not aware of your feelings, your life is lived incompletely. Whenever you don't feel, you are blocked from living life to the fullest."[18]

The journey to wholeness will require that we begin to live authentically from our hearts, where we embrace our feelings. Avoiding our feelings is the norm for many people. It leads us to isolation and ultimately to different forms of masking those feelings. These deeply ingrained patterns of avoiding our feelings begin to rule our lives and can lead to unhealthy behaviors. To become free from these behaviors, we must learn a new response to these feelings. That begins by understanding the tremendous value that God gave us through feelings. And as we learn to live from our hearts, feeling these feelings, we can begin the path to wholeness.

EXPLORING THE FEELINGS CHART

In his book, *Voice of the Heart,*[19] Dr. Chip Dodd explores the eight core feelings that we all experience in the human condition and how they help us purely experience and understand the depth of our hearts. It is important to learn to name feelings as a part of this healing process.

There is power in identifying and understanding the eight feelings. They are: hurt, loneliness, sadness, anger, fear, shame, guilt, and gladness. Many people often look at this list of feelings (also referred to as the Feelings Chart[20]) and ask, "Why is only one feeling positive and all the others are negative?" The truth is that all eight feelings are good. Each feeling is positive because of where it can lead. Each feeling has its own specific purpose in helping us live life fully.

In his book, *Journey to Freedom,* Scott Reall says, "In recovery I do choose to feel my feelings; that means often having to feel pain. That pain will let me feel my feelings. I had to let them teach me, allow God to use them, and let me live from my heart and not use the various forms of avoidance that I was medicating with. We must learn not to avoid and escape our feelings. If we do we will miss the greatest gift that they can bring us: freedom."[21]

Our journey to wholeness must take us through our feelings. Our feelings must be embraced and be processed if we are to find freedom and fullness of life. When we avoid our feelings—by medicating, becoming depressed, or whatever that response is—we are going to stay stuck.

Let's look deeper at Dr. Dodd's eight feelings and at how each one both benefits us on our journey when we allow ourselves to feel and the impairments that we experience when we do not allow ourselves to feel.

BENEFITS

Hurt leads to healing.

It is important that we identify what has hurt us. If we can identify that hurt, it will lead us to what is causing the pain, which will in turn guide us in the process of healing. Just think about when you go into a doctor's office: the first thing that he or she asks you is, "Where does it hurt?" The doctor cannot give you an assessment or make you feel better until knowing what the problem is. It is the same with our pain. We cannot begin to heal until we admit that we were hurt. Then and only then can we deal with it. Dr. Dodd says, "For in the admission to hurt you also expose yourself to healing."[22]

Loneliness moves us to intimacy.

Loneliness exposes us to our hunger for relationships. If we will respond to loneliness in a healthy way, it will require us to take the initiative to be authentic with people. We will have to embrace the idea of being known and earnestly seek out relationships. God gave us this natural feeling so that we may use it to draw closer to him/her, others, and ourselves.

Sadness expresses value and honor.

Sadness reveals how much we value something that we have lost. Sadness, if we will embrace it, reveals just how much we cared about something or someone. Sadness can show us just how valuable something was in our lives so that we might give it the honor that it deserves.

Anger hungers for life.

Anger lets my heart know that which really, truly matters to me. Anger can reveal how much my heart is affected by something that failed to happen. It can move us to go out and make a difference in our life and the lives of others. One of the best examples that I can think of is the first time that Jesus got really angry in the Bible.[23] He came upon money changers making a mockery of God's holy place. Jesus expressed his great displeasure and cleared out those who were insulting all that he stood for. He saw what they were doing to such a precious and sacred place, and he acted out of passion for His Father. Anger shows how passionately something matters to us. It is the energy that can propel us to go out and do something that matters and truly make a difference.

Fear awakens us to danger and begins wisdom.
Fear is a healthy emotion. It will awaken us to the many consequences that can happen from one simple act. Fear makes us see the dangerous possibilities of our actions and will guide us to wisdom in making future decisions. Fear can provide a sense of accountability and can motivate us to move in a new direction. Healthy fear always leads to the beginning of wisdom.

Shame maintains humility and mercy.
Shame shows us that we cannot do everything; that we have limitations. It shows us that we are not God. Shame does not humiliate; it helps create humility within us. It should be a relief to know that we cannot and are not expected to do everything. Healthy shame leads me to identify that I am human, make mistakes, and need help.

Guilt brings forgiveness.
Guilt is what we feel when we do something wrong. It is all about behavior and actions. Guilt comes from actions that I did when I harmed someone or actions that I should have taken when I did not. If we listen to the guilt, we become aware of how we acted and know that we must make the situation or relationship right. Guilt leads me to seek forgiveness so relationships can be restored.

Gladness proves the hope of the heart to be true.
Gladness is the result of allowing ourselves to feel the other seven feelings. It is great to feel these feelings because it means that our hearts are alive. If I feel my feelings and live from my heart, then I will know true gladness.

Gladness comes from being free. Dr. Gerald May says that only a free heart is really alive. That is what God wants. God does not want you bound, but free. Hearts that are in bondage to the control of their feelings are not free. Where there is no freedom, there is no gladness.

IMPAIRMENT

When we think of feelings as negative, it is often because we have experienced what Dr. Dodd calls the "impaired"[24] version of the feeling. This is what we experience when we don't allow ourselves to feel the true feeling. Just as each feeling has a "gift," each feeling has an impairment that comes when we do not allow ourselves to feel it.

Impaired Hurt: Resentment
Resentment is what happens when we try to avoid feeling hurt. Resentment deflects our focus away from our internal pain and on to someone or something else. Hurt most often comes in relationships, and God brings healing to where there has been hurt through relationships. God wants us to be vulnerable about the relationship that is causing us pain. Only then can God heal our heart and move us forward.

Impaired Loneliness: Apathy
Apathy is the opposite of love. It says, "I just don't care anymore." If I refuse to feel loneliness, it will drive me inward even further into isolation and depression and possibly to forms of unhealthy coping. I can let my loneliness keep me from ever seeking out relationships and let it control my everyday activities for fear of letting people know me.

Impaired Sadness: Self-Pity
We often fear expressing sadness because we don't want to be seen as having self-pity. But in actuality true sadness and self-pity are very different. Dr. Dodd defines self-pity as "a way to escape the pain of sadness by trying to make others feel sadness for us." If I am unwilling

to feel sadness myself, I may try to get someone else to feel what I refuse to feel. This will not cleanse my heart and bring healing. I must allow myself to feel the depth of the loss and the sadness that comes from losing someone or something that I value.

Impaired Anger: Depression

Depression has often been defined as anger turned inward. It also occurs when I close off my desires and passions. The energy of anger is turned against myself, and I become worn out. I have no motivation, no energy, no passion—and no vision for my life. True anger is a good thing—it expresses our desire for life. This is different from how we may have thought about anger before, as uncontrollable rage. Rage is not an impairment of anger, but an impairment of fear.

Impaired Fear: Anxiety/Control/Rage:

Fear will drive us in one of two directions: it can drive us to faith and surrendering our lives to God's care, or it will drive us to try to control our circumstances in an attempt to avoid the negative event that we fear. When we experience anxiety, we may be experiencing unresolved events of our lives that trigger a feeling of being unsafe, unloved or abandoned, and we may need help to work through these complex reactions. When we are anxious, we often try to control the people and circumstances of our lives to conform to our expectations and needs so we can feel secure. When they do not conform and we are unable to control them, we can react in rage. Rage destroys the benefit of fear because it is a refusal to face our fear of vulnerability to the point that it denies the fact that fear exists. Most people confuse rage and anger— we think that they are the same thing, when they really could not be further apart.

Dr. Dodd puts it this way: "Rage rejects the fear of having desire. Anger is an acknowledgment of the depth of our desire."[25] If you struggle with rage, the question that you need to ask yourself is not "what am I angry about?" but rather, "what am I so afraid of?"

Impaired Shame: Toxic Shame

When I believe that I am flawed and defective as a human being, then I have moved away from a state of healthy shame, and I constantly condemn and criticize myself. We call this toxic shame, and it is what drives the inner critic and negative thinking. It is where I have taken shame on as an identity—I am ashamed of who I am. It drives me to humiliation, which says "You are so bad," and away from my need for God and others.

Impaired Guilt: Pride/Toxic Shame

It is very dangerous when I do not feel guilt. If I do not feel remorse in my heart when I have done something wrong, then I will not seek forgiveness and relationships will remain fractured. Pride keeps us from asking for forgiveness because it rejects our true condition and refuses to be vulnerable to another person. In order not to feel guilt, we may blame others and justify our own actions so that we don't have to feel our own hurt. We can also go the other direction with guilt, and feel that we are not just guilty of a bad action—we are all bad. Toxic shame rejects the forgiveness of others and continues to feel bad even after we have sought forgiveness.

Impaired Gladness: Happiness/Entertainment

Happiness has its root in the word happenstance, which means that circumstances are what dictate our happiness. In an attempt to manufacture joy, we look to external events to bring us the happiness that we all desire. Yet haven't you found that those events never seem to quite fulfill your expectations? We are left with a sense of wanting more. While pleasurable activities can be good things, they are temporary pleasures, which will not bring true, lasting fulfillment. We need to be aware of whether these activities are fueled by a need to escape our feelings, and whether we are engaging in them too frequently. If we are not finding fulfillment in feeling and owning all of our feelings in relationships, then these things end up being distractions that take us away from our heart rather than into our heart.

REFLECTIONS

1. What are the feelings you have experienced throughout your diagnosis and treatment?

2. Are there feelings that you don't believe you have permission to feel or express? Why?

3. After studying the benefit of each feeling, how has that changed your view of a particular feeling that otherwise may have been viewed as negative?

BREAKING THE CHAIN
OF NEGATIVE THOUGHTS

When our first thought upon waking in the morning and the last thought before we go to sleep at night is, "I have cancer," it can set the stage for brooding, or dwelling on the negative. The thing to remember is this: while we can't control the thoughts that pop into our mind, we can control what we do with those thoughts. One survivor shared a therapist's advice that you can't stop a bird from flying through your head but you can stop it from building a nest. We can change our paradigm.

This may be a time when our inner critic may be more active than before. The feeling of being vulnerable in life can bring up doubts about so many things. But we have a choice. We can wander into that dark cavern, where we feel like we're flawed and defective. Or, we can counter negative thoughts with ones that are more positive. Once we fall into the trap of brooding, it's easy to link several bad occurrences together—like having been excluded in high school, losing a job, experiencing a divorce—or whatever struggles have been experienced throughout life. These losses, when linked together, can collectively create feelings of worthlessness. We begin to believe our whole life can be summed up by these events.

If we focus on the negative—that our body let us down, that our partner or spouse will never find us attractive again, that we are somehow to blame for getting cancer—we will spiral down a tunnel that can be very difficult to crawl out of. This is not to say that we won't ever have these thoughts. The key is how we respond to them when they occur. Looking for even one small thing for which to be grateful can be a powerful step in breaking the chain of negative thoughts.

I first met Dawn a week before she started chemo, so she was in the limbo of waiting, trying hard to calm the fear of the unknown. She confided that yes, she had moments that were close to panic—but she also had moments of gratefulness and beauty. "I was driving the other day and suddenly realized how bright and warm the sunshine was. I felt the comfortable hardness of the steering wheel, and I was grateful that I had something in my control, that I could appreciate the beauty of the world around me, that I have access to good healthcare. In a moment, the dread evaporated. I realized that my whole perspective had shifted, at least for that space of time."

What Dawn discovered is a universal truth: gratefulness and negative thoughts cannot exist together at the same time. By acknowledging her feeling of being grateful for simple things like the sun shining, and then a bigger thing like having access to good healthcare, Dawn replaced a negative thought with a positive one. As unnatural and forced as it may seem, if we can make ourselves say "thank you," for the small things, it causes us to become closer to the Spirit within. This, in turn, essentially takes our mind off the negative as we focus on that for which we are grateful. Some days that may only be that we wake up breathing, but it's a start.

I've read Sarah Young's book, *Jesus Calling,*[26] daily for the last several years, and her gratitude practice has become my practice. I can testify that being grateful truly does become easier and more natural the more I work on finding things throughout each day for which I can be thankful. Gratefulness is the sunshine that drives out the darkness of negative thoughts.

On the other hand, we may experience genuine sadness during this time. Sadness is very different from negative thinking, in that it is actually honoring the present moment with the real changes and loss it brings. Sadness doesn't call into question our worth or point blame. It acknowledges what is happening now is difficult. We can experience sadness and still be living in immense gratitude for our lives. As author Ann Voscamp points out, "It's a strange thing to find out your heart can explode with love and suffering and find out they're kin in ways we don't care to admit. I don't know how to put all these broken pieces back into place. Maybe that's the point?" Sadness allows us to take care of our broken pieces rather than telling us we are weak for having broken pieces. And in this acceptance, we keep moving emotionally instead of getting stuck in the negative.

REFLECTIONS

1. When you experience sadness, do you give yourself permission to feel it fully?

2. Has your self-image been challenged by your diagnosis? If so, how?

3. What do you find yourself grateful for these days?

LIVING YOUR AUTHENTIC SELF

*Authenticity is the daily practice of letting go
of who we think we're supposed to be,
and embracing who we are.*

—BRENÉ BROWN

UNDERSTANDING TOXIC SHAME

Toxic shame is an experience all humans have encountered. It is being told or treated as if we are hopelessly flawed, inadequate, worthless or unlovable. It involves feeling rejected, humiliated, exposed. We may have experienced this kind of shame at home, at school, at work or in friendships or romantic relationships. We have had a brief encounter with toxic shame or continual exposure to it. Our level of exposure significantly influences our paradigm, our inner critic and our ability to extend self-compassion. The overcoming of this requires work.

Inside each of us, there is an inner critic that reminds us of our frailty and faults. Some of the inner criticism stems from something in our past. A cancer survivor, Morgan, had parents who divorced when she was very young, and her mother worked long hours to support them.

Morgan and her brother were often left alone with chores and homework to finish, and if these weren't done to their mother's satisfaction there were harsh consequences. The children felt that no matter what they did, they never lived up to their mother's expectations. There was a series of boyfriends, resulting in even less attention, until the mother eventually remarried and Morgan finally found what she called a "normal" family life.

As an adult, Morgan felt compelled to give everything 110 percent. "I wanted to be the perfect employee, the perfect wife, the perfect mother," she says, "but no matter how many hours I put in or how much I gave to others, I never felt like it was enough." When her children were in their late teens, she found the courage to divorce her verbally abusive husband and began taking care of her ailing mother. Then came her cancer diagnosis. "I was exhausted, and I was devastated," Morgan recalls. "But I just put on my happy face and kept on working full time, tending to Mom, supporting my children, everything I'd always done. I felt like I'd be a failure if I stopped anything." She met a wonderful man but her inner critic told her she wasn't worthy of his love. She felt unattractive physically and inferior in every way.

Morgan's story is a powerful example of what happens when we carry negative messages inside us from childhood. Sometimes we have a happy childhood but then find ourselves in unhealthy relationships at work or in marriage. It really doesn't take many years of hearing negative messages to start believing them. Sadly, the volume dial of the negative messages many times seems to be turned up louder than the volume of the positive ones.

Fear is what gives shame its strength. Deep inside all of us lurks the suspicion or fear that if we allow our true selves to be known, we will be found lacking, unlovable or defective. Shame originates inside each of us from some sort of system: a family system, church system, education system, for example. Over the course of our lives we develop a myriad of coping mechanisms to be able to live with this constant companion. We may become "people pleasers," doing and saying what we think others want instead of taking care of our own needs.

Learning to say "no" has become a popular theme in today's culture, when in fact the better practice is to say what we really feel and what we really mean with compassionate honesty.

People pleasing can take many forms in many different areas of our life. Most are easy to recognize, even if it's difficult to admit. Other forms are more subtle. As women, we tend to be nurturers and caregivers. After a cancer diagnosis we see the worry in the faces of those who love us, and we feel a need to be strong for them even when we long to express our own concerns and lean on someone for support. We fear, perhaps unconsciously, that others will see us as weak or less than perfect in some way if we let them know who we really are and how we're really feeling. The outpouring of kindness: meals delivered, rides to treatment, friends who clean the house, neighbors who take the kids on playdates, can be especially hard to accept.

On the one hand, we feel loved and valued. On the other, we want to be strong and in control. We fear we are being pitied because we can't do all that we did before. But consider this: most of us delight in helping others. We're uncomfortable accepting it, but in reality we're giving our friends and loved ones a gift by allowing them to care for us. We can choose to respond to this situation by expressing our gratitude and learning what is most helpful to others when their time of need arises. On the other end of the spectrum, we may find that family or friends don't react as expected. They may dismiss the diagnosis as insignificant, or worry only how it will affect their own lives. This apparent lack of concern can be very hurtful.

Emotional pain is a part of life, and it's likely that we've developed strategies to deal with it along our life's journey. It's natural to want to avoid pain, so we learn to disconnect from it. When we disconnect from our true selves, feelings and needs, we turn to other things to fill the void. We form attachments in many ways, even to things that are perceived as good—work, fitness, cleanliness, shopping, eating, approval, relationships, ambition, goals, being busy or active. We put our identity in these things rather than living out our true self.

Another way we cope with pain is by "stuffing" it. Instead of working through it, we cover it with a scab called the false self. It only takes one mistake, one put-down by another, one lost relationship, and the scab peels away. What is left is a wounded feeling of unhealthy shame. This feeling isolates us as we journey through life. Our inner critic gives specifics to our secret fears, and we may eventually come to believe that we are flawed and worthless. This is what we call toxic shame; we have become ashamed of who we are.

Toxic shame injures our relationships. We can't be emotionally close to anyone if we've closed off our true self. We cannot fully love others without loving ourselves first. We turn to objects, such as expensive houses or cars, designer clothing, or the next promotion at work, in an effort to fulfill our loneliness. We believe that if we can get more and more stuff, it will finally be enough. It never is. Relating to the world on this level never makes us feel loved for who we are, but for how we look, how we perform, or by what we own. This defense mechanism helps for a while, but it eventually wears us down.

But like all emotions, shame has a benefit as well as an impairment. The benefit of shame is that it gives us humility and the freedom to say, "I'm human. I make mistakes. I need help."

Toxic shame is overcome by grace, God's unmerited mercy and divine assistance to and for us. Author Richard Rohr describes grace as "...what God does to keep all things God has made in love and alive—forever. Grace is God's official job description. Grace is not something God gives; grace is who God is."[27]

Grace allows us to know that we are not alone. We are not hopeless. Imperfection is an unavoidable part of the human condition. We are, each of us, flawed. Rather than projecting a false image of our lives, grace allows us to recognize that humans are connected by our imperfections.

As we were nearing the end of our time together, Morgan confided to her fellow survivors, "The first time I sat with you and saw all these smiling faces, I just knew that everyone else had it together and I would be the only one with issues. But what I've found is that we're all a little flawed, and we love each other anyway!" It's true—we are all perfectly imperfect!

When we can change our narrative to embrace, if not celebrate, our shortcomings, we create an opportunity to connect with others. Our paradigm shifts happen with time and in baby steps, moving us toward the benefit side of shame. Here we let go of the past. We recognize that we can't change it, but we can reframe the story we tell ourselves about the past. We can learn from those experiences and use that wisdom to become better versions of ourselves.

One of the best parts of the small group process—it allows us to simply be. We all crave connection at our core. There aren't many opportunities in life to be able to sit with others and say, without judgment, "I don't have it together." It's been said that "it's impossible to be your best self by yourself." Small groups give us an opportunity to experience reassurance and healing in our togetherness. It also gives us the opportunity to be self-reflective. "As Carl Jung stated, "Who looks outside dreams; who looks inside, awakes."[28]

REFLECTIONS

1. What was your loudest toxic shame message?

2. "Should" is a shaming word. What are the "shoulds" in your life coming from yourself and/or others?

3. Name past mistakes or regrets that you need to let go of to begin healing.

YOUR TRUE SELF

We all feel the call of our authentic, true selves some time in our lives. The person we were created to be. We may not even know exactly what that means. Most of us can't recall a time when we "knew" our self-identity outside the context of our relationships with family or friends. It's gotten all caught up in our experiences, our performance culture, constant decision-making and the frantic pace of everyday life. In every way, we are forced by life to take a journey away from ourselves and then back again. But the good news is we can be better if we are willing to do the inner, emotional work. Likely we have felt unexplained whispers, nudges, or desires to follow a call toward our authentic self throughout our lifetime. We just may not have recognized it alongside the many other voices in our lives.

Gerald May refers to this inner spiritual voice as "the longing."[29] It is a deep awareness of ourselves, much deeper than a call to a certain career or project or creative task. It's a sense of who we are, stripped down from all the ways that we describe ourselves or others perceive us.

Richard Rohr calls it the "immortal diamond,"[30] that hard-to-find the inner nugget of who we are. The part of us that is more connected to the divine than to being human. It is always there. It has been there from the start, and it is God in us and we in God. Our lifetime task is to rediscover it and hold onto it.

It is often a crisis like a life-threatening disease that allows us to be more open to that distant inner voice that tells us life is so much bigger than we really understand. In the previous chapters, we've talked about making meaning out of our suffering, of finding purpose, of recalibrating our lives to stop wasting time. But often we still put those ideas in the context of "doing" something…like starting a job, leaving a job, spending more time with others, pursuing a hobby, being more creative, taking better care of ourselves, learning a new skill.

One survivor said she thought her identity was what she did. She saw herself as a wife, a mom, a grandmother, an employee. But those are her roles in life, not who she is. She realized she is a person who is fun-loving, friendly, a Christian, a nature lover and adventurous. **That** is who she **is**.

Perhaps the best thing that we can do for ourselves first is to let the rawness of this moment expose our beautiful and untouched inner core. To slow down and ask the burning question, who am I outside all of this? Outside my experiences, outside my successes, my setbacks, my struggles, my roles? Sometimes it helps to just picture yourself as a child, totally innocent and infinitely curious about the world. This is who you still are, deep down. If we can refind our true selves, it will anchor us through all the storms of life. This is the time to reclaim yourself.

Realize you are not obligated to play by other people's rules. There is no prerequisite for you to manage any life "edits" toward a perfectionism that simply never exists. This is your life and you are the only you—ever. Touch base with yourself to find the true you, right now. Ways to realize your true self could include:

Ask yourself what you need
Stand up for yourself
Reconnect with your joy
Return to your "center"
Follow your curiosity
Be even just a little bit more vulnerable
Journal
Accept your "good"

Let go of any grudges you may be holding against yourself for whatever reason
Follow your heart
Acknowledge your true feelings and own them
Practice more self love
Seek professional help if needed
Connect with others—seek meaningful connections
Set healthy boundaries

If we can refind our true selves, it will anchor us through all the storms of life. This is the time to be present in the here and now. The time to align your actions with your values. The time to find that true core of who you are and allow for more genuine acceptance. This is the time to reclaim yourself.

REFLECTIONS

1. Describe yourself as a child. Who were you? What were your likes
   and dislikes? What were you interested in or curious about?

2. What parts of your childhood self can you still identify? What
   parts have you "put away" or "hidden"?

3. List some of your roles. Now describe who you are outside of your
   roles.

THE CREATIVE SELF

The world we live in is an amazingly complex, colorful and fascinating place. It reflects the creative energy and genius that made it. It tells us something about the infinite amount of new ideas just waiting to be birthed. Just thinking about a creator that can make the earth and the universe gives me hope. If that is possible, anything is possible.

That same creative energy flows through us. After all, we are part of this amazing place!

Why is this important now, in the face of something like a cancer diagnosis? Because you are on a journey that holds so much possibility, to reclaim your true self and reclaim your creative life. It all comes back to hope. Creating is hope.

Most of us have quieted our creative selves because we have narrowed the definition of creative to something very small and limiting. We think we must be a painter, or be able to draw or make music. We forget that there are many ways to live creatively. Being creative means finding new solutions, new perspectives, new processes. Julia Cameron says, "Creativity is an experience—to my eye, a spiritual experience. It does not matter which way you think of it: creativity leading to spirituality or spirituality leading to creativity. In fact, I do not make a distinction between the two."[31]

Our true selves and our creative selves are one in the same. If we can reclaim one, we reclaim the other. There is urgency now to reflect on what needs to happen in our lives to get there. Sharing our life story with others is a great start. We start to make sense of our experiences and find connection in our human condition. What else do we need to do? Perhaps it is more inner reflective work. Perhaps it is a spiritual practice or direction. Maybe we need to self-care and create a different rhythm in our lives. Or we can find simple ways to unblock our creative spirit by journaling, writing, drawing, painting, photography, scrapbooking, gardening or whatever brings us joy. The point is to form a deeper connection with the flow in the universe that connects us all and to open your life to its most potential.

REFLECTIONS

1. In what ways are you creative?

2. What would you do more of if you could?

3. Is there something you are repeatedly drawn to that you'd love to try?

FACING MIDLIFE

Interestingly, the average age of a breast cancer diagnosis tends to coincide with midlife, which brings with it its own issues. Midlife is often its own total paradigm shift. We start to feel our age, question our purpose, ask the question, "Is this it? Is this all there is?" Nothing is truly certain or predictable. We are acutely aware that we are not exempt from suffering. Life has pushed us around; we've taken our punches; we feel more tired, sometimes resigned. Brené Brown describes this as a "midlife unraveling". She says, "Whatever the issue, it seems as if we spend the first half of our lives shutting down feelings to stop the hurt, and the second half trying to open everything back up to heal the hurt... After two decades of research on shame, authenticity, and belonging, I'm convinced that loving ourselves is the most difficult and courageous thing we'll ever do. Maybe we've been given a finite amount of time to find that self-love, and midlife is the halfway mark. It's time to let go of the shame and fear and embrace love. Time to fish or cut bait."[32] Self love is a choice we can make.

On the other hand, breast cancer is definitely a crisis—it is an intense, acute event. Maybe it speeds up the typical mid-life unraveling because we are forced to listen to the universe earlier than we might otherwise. Or maybe it forces us to recognize that we are vulnerable physically, and so we are more ready to look at our emotional vulnerability. A cancer diagnosis can most definitely be a rebirth.

The experience of cancer accentuates the issues of midlife. It is incredibly hard in the midst of a cancer diagnosis to know what emotions, fears, insecurities, questions and changes we might have experienced just as part of the paradigm shift of midlife anyway or whether they are exclusively because of our circumstances. This is why it's so important to not give cancer credit for all we may be facing. We don't have to be victims of cancer. Maybe we'd be experiencing these things in our lives without our diagnosis. Everything can't be blamed on cancer. It's a perspective shift. One survivor mentioned in her small group that she didn't think cancer deserved that much respect.

In some ways, we can take comfort in knowing that we are not alone in these questions, these feelings. We may say to ourselves, "Why don't I see the world like I used to? Am I becoming cynical? Things just don't make as much sense anymore." In truth, we are shifting into a different season of life. We are different. Our bodies are different. And that is okay.

In this season, we can become better at self-love. In many ways, we have exhausted the ambitions of our younger years: to meet others' standards for us and for what defines "success." We can start to feel comfortable with who we are and embrace our struggles, our stories and our strengths. In fact, this disquieting season can emerge, as we have said before, as a new time of creativity and chance-taking as we embrace that we have experienced and learned a lot. We are moving toward the wisdom, discernment and perspective that only comes with age. This emerging may still be painful and uncertain, but we need to just keep moving forward, one day at a time, and keep asking the question, "What does God have for me now?"

REFLECTIONS

1. Before your cancer diagnosis, had you already experienced any of the normal shifts of midlife? For example, changes in your body, your relationships, your view of what is important in life?

2. Brené Brown says that "loving ourselves is the most difficult and courageous thing we'll ever do." What do you think this means?

3. What, if anything, have you given cancer credit for that could be a part of normal mid-life happenings?

NO MORE GAMES

After spending most of our lives building walls to guard our authentic selves, we realize that life's too short to keep playing games. We've survived losing our hair, our breasts, our privacy, our sense of femininity, our energy and vitality, our sense of safety, and quite possibly a few folks we once called friends. After all that, it becomes easier to tell the world, "Here I am, warts and all. Take me or leave me, but this is who I am."

Now is the time to commit to the one person whose intimacy you need the most—yourself. We forget that we journey this life mostly alone, but we're always in our own psychological headspace. It's not fair to hope for others to fill up our tanks—it is not anyone else's job. Having a good and committed relationship with ourselves is the foundation for having a good and committed relationship with others.

Charlotte was thirty-eight when I met her. A single, professional woman, she exuded confidence and had a wry sense of humor that always brought a laugh to any conversation. She dismissed her diagnosis as "just a little cancer" and blew off her lumpectomy and radiation as "no big deal, just an annoyance really." Charlotte's intention was to engage in a breast cancer recovery program to work back up to her former level of advanced interval training.

"I thought it would be fun to meet other women who might turn into new workout buddies," she remembers. "I thought maybe I could help someone else. I wasn't at all prepared for how fatigued I was; how difficult it was now to do things I used to do as a warm-up."

This made her feel anger, shame, sadness and hurt—but she hid those feelings behind her jokes. This beautiful, strong, competent, confident woman was wrestling with an identity crisis that she refused to acknowledge.

"I liked my life just fine the way it was," she said. "I thought everything was under control. I didn't see a need to make any changes."

Then we ran those darn stairs together, sweated and cussed our trainer together, swore off sugar together. We met each week just to talk in our small group, and each week we all shared a little more of ourselves. It was like a curtain was lifting and we started to see the real people behind the marionettes. I had a secret that I'd never shared with anyone before. It hurt so bad for so long that I buried it... I buried it deep. Then one night in our group that secret, that pain, just jumped right out of my mouth. I think I was as surprised as everyone else, but the words just kept pouring out while every single person listened. I felt respected. There was no judgment. They even let me cry, and when I was through I still felt loved by every one of those women. The secret lost its power over me once I got it out. That's when I truly became whole," Charlotte concluded. "That's when I finally understood the journey."

REFLECTIONS

1. How does keeping secrets impact your emotional well being?

2. What are secrets in your life that you are tired of carrying? Are you ready to let go of them?

3. Complete the following thought. Take me or leave me, but this is what's true about me right now:

WHAT IS YOUR WHY?

If you've spent time around children, you know that they go through a stage when "why?" is their favorite word. This natural curiosity can wear out a parent's nerves after a while, but it's a necessary part of human development. It's how we begin to understand the world around us, and also the world within us… why is the grass green; why does Mommy cry?

Sadly, most of us lose this curiosity—or least stop questioning—as we get older. If we can tap into our inner preschooler and learn to look for the "why," we can often discover much about our inner selves. When we're contemplating making a change, there is a process called Five Questions that can help us get to the core of our desire. This in turn helps reveal our true motivation. As we've discussed, intrinsic motivation will carry us longer and farther toward lasting change than extrinsic, or external, motivation.

If you are contemplating change; if you are restless and unsettled; if you want your life to be different… why? That's the first level, but it rarely gives us the real answer. We often need to confront whatever emotional pain is making us want a change and then take concrete action steps in order to achieve real, lasting transformation.

Ellen tried to complete a breast cancer recovery program four times in the last six years. Every time, she quit after one or two workouts. The last time she came in, we talked about her goals… again.

"What do you want to get out of this program?" I asked.

"I'm tired of being tired," Ellen said. "I just want to lose weight and feel fit again." "How long have you wanted this?" I asked.

Ellen looked surprised, but then confessed that she's been fighting weight gain since before her diagnosis. Her oncologist had been urging her to lose the extra pounds since finishing chemo, and now her primary care physician had warned that her pre-diabetes was about to drop the "pre" and require medication if she didn't drop 20 pounds.

"How does that make you feel?" I asked.

It took a moment for Ellen to answer, but then she told me her mother was overweight and had diabetes. "I feel like I'm following in her footsteps."

"I know you have a close, loving relationship with your mother," I replied. "Why does that bother you?" The tears began to flow as Ellen told me that her daughter would no longer allow her to babysit her children. "She said I'm too overweight and immobile to keep up with them. I'm just heartbroken. And so embarrassed. I should have taken better care of myself and not let my weight get so out of hand!"

By asking "why" and digging deeper, by discovering the real source of her pain, Ellen found her true motivation. When goals are vague and superficial, such as "feeling better," or "getting healthy," ask the next level of "why?" to get to the root of what you're truly looking for.

Scientists believe that when the Titanic approached the iceberg, the captain turned the ship to avoid hitting it. But the largest part of the iceberg was underwater, and it tore a gaping hole all along the side of the ship, causing it to sink. It is believed that if the Titanic would have hit the iceberg head-on, the ship would have been crippled, but it would not have sunk because that is how ships are made to take impact.

Don't be like the Titanic and sidestep your pain. Hit it head on. Dig into it. Don't let hidden pain fuel your inner critic or keep you from living the life you deserve.

The reality is that Ellen had started a program designed to help participants achieve better lifestyle habits no less than four times. Now that she had pinpointed her true motivation, she set out to discover what had been holding her back. After much reflection, she uncovered the pain that was undermining her efforts: a deep fear of not being good enough. If she couldn't do it perfectly, she wouldn't do it at all.

If any of this sounds familiar, remember that change doesn't happen overnight. As you slowly open the door to your authentic self, take baby steps. Do one small thing that you can feel good about. If you want to change your lifestyle, set a goal you can easily achieve... first, walk for 15 minutes twice a week. Then add a third day. Then increase one day to 30 minutes. You get the idea. Once you've perfected that one thing, add something else. Share your pain, your motivation, and your goals with someone you trust. Allow them to help you. As you make progress, give yourself grace not to be perfect... no human is.

REFLECTIONS

Using the five questions below, what is the deep root of your "why?*
(This is just an example; use whatever scenario fits your situation.)

1. Why do I want to change my eating and exercise habits? (Because I want to lose weight)

2. Why do I want to lose weight? (Because I want my clothes to fit better.)

3. Why do I want my clothes to fit better? (Because I want to feel proud of who I am.)

4. Why do I want to feel proud of who I am? (Living in a way that makes me proud to be me means living a long, healthy life.)

5. Why is it important to me to live a long, healthy life? (There's more I want to accomplish. And I'm scared I won't be around for my kids when they need me the most.)

* Keep asking "why" until you find your compelling reason.

RELATIONSHIP WITH OTHERS AND OURSELVES

"Would you be my neighbor?"
—FRED ROGERS

*"Self-esteem is about trusting our ability
to make appropriate choices
and cope effectively with adversity."*
—DR. NATHANIAL BRANDON

*"Never doubt that a small group of thoughtful people
can change the world.
Indeed, that is the only thing that ever has."*
—MARGARET MEAD

"Forgiveness is the greatest gift you can give yourself."
—MAYA ANGELOU

*"People do not decide their future.
They decide their habits.
And it's their habits that decide their future."*
—F.M. ALEXANDER

RELATIONSHIPS ON THE JOURNEY

Universality. That's a term that means "we are not alone." Others have issues that are much like ours. We struggle together. When we see others struggle with similar problems, it draws us out of isolation and into a place of safety. In the company of others with comparable experiences, we can discover healing.

One of the greatest truths about growth and healing is that "I can't do it alone." I need others. I need their support. I need their encouragement. I need their love. I need their accountability. Most people will not abandon us or reject us if we become honest and confess our struggles. Most will meet us in our pain and comfort us.

Breast cancer can be an isolating experience. No one else can feel what you feel physically, emotionally, or spiritually. From the moment we hear the words, "You have cancer," we begin to realize that it is our yoke to bear. Our support system can love us, to be sure, but it is our own personal experience. Well-meaning family and friends may tell us how to walk down our path. But it's our journey alone and we have to decide what works for ourselves. It may be the first time we haven't been able to share openly with our spouse, partner, parents, siblings, or children—we want to shield them from the pain and the scary stuff. Our loved ones want us to be okay so they can be okay. So life will roll on as it did before. But since they can't feel what we feel, it's difficult for them to be empathetic and easy for them to misunderstand why we have chemo brain, or why we aren't back to our old selves as soon as we finish treatment. That's why sharing with other survivors is so helpful—we share a common experience that is difficult for others to fully understand.

I remember leaving my oncologist's office one day and stopping by the store on my way home. I was standing in front of the paper towels when she called with some test results. While half my brain tried to comprehend what she was telling me, the other half went floating off and watched the moments unfold like a spectator at a play. That half of my brain saw that everyone else in the store was totally oblivious to me and my phone call. I realized that the world would keep turning no matter what personal tragedy was unfolding, and I felt more alone than I'd ever felt in my life.

Universality creates one of the greatest dynamics in healing—a place of safety and compassion. When I come out of isolation and connect with a community of people who have struggled the same way I have, who have felt the same things I have felt, and who want the same things I want, this is the journey to wholeness. This is grace.

As women, most of us are hard-wired to intuitively seek out community. We seem to instinctively know that we will find comfort, wisdom, and healing in connection with others like ourselves. I was eight years out from my diagnosis when I started talking with the women entering a cancer recovery program. I listened to each of their stories and found a profound comfort and, ultimately, healing, in sharing mine with them. I didn't even realize I needed that, but over the course of the next few years I gradually came to a place of acceptance. Unfortunately some prefer to avoid—pretend like it didn't happen. They think this is moving on, but it is not. Putting it out there is cathartic. There is so much power in sharing our stories in a community of others with similar experiences!

Through this sharing of experiences with other survivors, I felt the truth in the words that listening is the greatest gift that we can give and receive. In any relationship, listening encourages open discussion. We must never judge people when we are listening to them. The fact that they are telling you their truth is important, so affirm that in an encouraging, nonjudgmental way, just like we do in small group. It helps to know that we aren't alone. Most of the time we don't want advice, we just need caring friendship.

Soon after my diagnosis, my neighbor, who I barely knew, hosted a hat and scarf party for me. Not only did my friends show up, but so did most of the neighborhood—even women I knew only by name. And they all wore hats! This was the beginning of an outpouring of kindness and love that completely changed my life. I finally realized that I didn't need to be perfect… these people cared about me just the way I was, which at the time was weepy, bald, unemployed, and sometimes too tired to mother my kids. Their acts of kindness let me know that I was enough. It was a show of true community.

Outside our "sisterhood," we need to remember that effective communication is vital to all our relationships. This is often easier said than done. Communication sometimes has a way of breaking down between people. The stress of a cancer diagnosis can make it easier to retreat than to be vulnerable and open. Relationships can be challenging—but they may be one of the most decisive factors in our process of change. Our recovery, our healing, our future may very well come down to those with whom we associate and how we relate to our loved ones. Supportive relationships help us own our stories and move forward.

REFLECTIONS

1. Have you been in community or in isolation since your
   diagnosis? Explain.

2. Who are the most important people in your community? Where
   are your gaps?

3. What are the hardest things for you to share about? The places
   you feel most vulnerable?

THE FREEDOM TO CHOOSE

Sadly, not all relationships are healthy. Psychologists Henry Cloud and John Townsend believe that we need people who can give and receive support, love, courage, feedback, wisdom, experience, and accountability.[33] These may be present in a relationship until cancer brings out fear and other emotions that can lead to disappointment and even heartbreak. "Sometimes the people you expect to show up for you don't or can't," many survivors note.

Women frequently say that after diagnosis they "find out who their real friends are." We may never know why people react to our diagnosis in a certain way. Maybe they simply do not know what to say or how to act. Or perhaps they are fighting their own past losses or fears, and possibly future fears. We find that some people we barely know or who we least expect step up and are surprisingly supportive. There may be those we believe we can count on who will literally or figuratively disappear. As our diagnosis orders our priorities, we may realize for the first time that not all our relationships are benefitting us. Some are one-sided at best, and toxic at worst. We will need to learn to grieve a change in our relationships as well.

This is also a chance for us to evaluate how we have acted in our relationships and perhaps do better in the future. We may realize that there have for too long been resentments, hurt, disagreements, and separation keeping us from closer relationships. We may realize we need to initiate connection more with others or heal wounds that are not worth holding onto anymore.

It has been said that some friends come into our lives for a reason. Others enter our lives for a season, some for a lifetime. Those who are there for a reason are the ones who appear suddenly during a crisis or other life event to provide support that only they have the ability to give. They have special gifts or talents or resources that you need and they are willing to share. They may also be the ones who stay silent during your crisis, teaching you valuable lessons that promote growth.

Those who are there for a season are the friends in your dorm at college, a set of co-workers, the young moms in your toddler's play group, and maybe the other cancer survivors you meet and share time with. They are the ones we share a specific life experience with. Sometimes they become lifetime friends and sometimes they don't, but their friendship serves a valuable purpose for the time it's there.

Lifetime friends are those who love us unconditionally and stick by us through decades. They are the ones you can call any time of the day or night to share joy or sorrow; the ones you know you can count on no matter what. They are there for weddings and divorce, for births and deaths, and for everything else life throws at us. We are blessed indeed to have a handful of lifetime friends, but we don't know which "reason" or "season" friends will become life-timers until they've been there that long.

Since most of our relationships are a choice, we have the freedom to disassociate with the unhealthy, toxic people in our lives. After going through a cancer experience, it seems that many of us gain a clarity that empowers even the most timid people-pleasers to end these toxic relationships. And if all the criteria for a healthy relationship (as defined by Cloud and Townsend) are present, our cancer experience may give us the ability to more freely make the choice as to whether or not we want to respond with understanding and forgiveness.

We can choose to recognize that the "reason" or "season" of someone's time in our life has ended, or put in the work to make it a lifetime friendship. We may learn that a relationship really is toxic and harmful to our happiness and well-being and choose to end it. Realizing that we have the freedom to choose, and acting on the choice that is most healthy for us, is one of the most freeing and empowering things we can do for ourselves.

REFLECTIONS

1. How have your relationships changed since your diagnosis?

2. Name a friend who was in your life for a reason or a season and share why.

3. What have you done about the relationships that aren't benefitting or haven't benefited you?

FORGIVENESS

If community feeds the soul, isolation kills the soul. Isolation is not the same as solitude. Solitude is being alone by choice, to renew ourselves, to think or connect spiritually. Isolation is being disconnected from others. Without the support of community—when we are in isolation—we begin to feel like we're the only ones who feel, think or experience things in a certain way.

Isolation distorts our perception, and that perception becomes our reality. The problem is no one is there to compassionately and honestly challenge our thinking. There's a saying that "a man who walks alone can talk himself into anything." The moral is: don't believe everything you think!

It is clear that to have physical, mental and spiritual health, humans need relationships with other humans. That's how God created us.

A part of universality that may be overlooked is that not only does it provide safety and comfort from a group of individuals who "get it," but it also helps us forgive ourselves. When we hear other people's stories, we can extend grace, mercy and compassion to them for the things they have done or experienced. Healing takes place as we then extend to ourselves the same compassion of forgiveness—something that can be a difficult thing to do. Sometimes we want to keep punishing ourselves. We beat ourselves up. But this can make us hopeless, bitter, and even more isolated. We need to deal with our problems first by becoming aware of them, and then by moving to a level of self-forgiveness.

To forgive ourselves means to live intentionally, making our own choices. Forgiveness in New Testament Greek means "to send away." So forgiveness becomes a conscious choice—we send away whatever issue we're dealing with, with no return address. You can even imagine yourself "gathering up" your forgiveness, placing it on a raft and watching it float away downstream. And all of this is easier when we're in community because there are others like us who can hold up the mirror, helping us see ourselves as we really are and not how we think we are.

As we've said before, we arrive at our diagnosis with a suitcase full of life experiences. That baggage shapes our inner narrative about who we are—the good and the bad. We're all human, and we all make mistakes. We may know that and still not be able to forgive ourselves. If our parents divorced when we were children, we may carry the guilt of thinking it's our fault even into adulthood. We may have used poor judgment in our teens and repeated the same mistake more than once, and then continue to beat ourselves up for it for decades. We may look back on our losses and feel like we caused one or more of them, and "got what we deserved." We may even think we somehow caused our cancer. Reasoning seems to fly out the window when we're in isolation, alone with our thoughts, and community gives us the chance to use the "say it out loud" test. Sometimes it just takes verbalizing thoughts to silence the inner critic so that we don't believe everything we think. And even if there are things in our lives that we need to practice healthy accountability around…if there are things that we need to apologize for, people to make amends to or reconciliation to be offered, community allows us to find the courage and perspective to move toward those.

When it comes to forgiving others it's important to understand what forgiveness is and what it is not. Forgiveness does not mean we're okay with the offense. Forgiveness does not mean that we'll never feel the pain of it again. Forgiveness is not forgetting. Forgiveness does not mean you have to restore a relationship. Forgiveness does not have to be asked for. Forgiveness is not a gift we give the other person, but it IS a gift we give ourselves. Forgiveness doesn't necessarily require a conversation. Forgiveness is a choice. Forgiveness is a deliberate decision to release feelings of resentment. Forgiveness is a matter of the heart.

Forgiveness is about living in the "now." The past has already happened. You can't change your past; you can only change the story you tell yourself and move forward.

REFLECTIONS

1. Name one thing you want to forgive yourself for. Is this something that is truly your responsibility or something that is actually someone else's responsibility?

2. Is there someone you are harboring bitterness or resentment toward?

3. How would it feel to forgive this person?

4. How might your problems or challenges be an opportunity for growth in your life?

THIS IS GETTING PERSONAL

After her bilateral mastectomy Susan had a very vivid dream. In this dream she was a man wearing camouflage and combat boots. Similar to a scene out of a war movie, she was desperately crawling through a small, tight tunnel. She was terrified and felt as if she couldn't breathe. There was panic at the thought of having to pull herself through the muddy, enclosed darkness. But she could see a hole at the end of the tunnel with light coming through. She knew she would have to force herself through the small hole, and was completely terrified to do so. But somehow she knew she would be ok if she could just force herself to get to the other side. She awoke from the dream in a full blown panic attack. Once she gained composure she shared the dream with her daughter, who immediately translated the dream. "Mom, don't you realize why you had that dream? You dreamt you were a man because you have no hair and no boobs right now. You were wearing camo and combat boots because you are in a fight for your life. The tunnel and the hole represent this breast cancer journey that you don't want to be taking. But Mom, you **will be okay** on the other side of it!" Susan wept at the magnitude of her subconscious fears but at the same time she was comforted. She knew she could do this, and even though her body was different now, she would be okay!

Cancer is the illness, but the disease is how it affects our life. We may feel as though our bodies betrayed us by becoming ill. If this is the case, we must forgive it. We need to extend to it the grace and compassion we would to anyone else. That said, it may take a long time to become friends with our new body. Reconstructed breasts merely sit on our chests; it may take years before they feel like anything but a foreign object, or they may not ever feel like a part of us. One of our group members explained, "They are **on me**, but they are not **of me**."

The scars and pain can be a continual reminder of our betrayal and loss. The lingering fatigue, achy joints, weight issues, lymphedema or the fear of developing it, changes in libido and physical sexual response can all change the relationship we have with our bodies. But forgiving the vessel in which we live and learning to give it compassion is the first step in becoming friends with the "new me."

One survivor shared with her JTW small group when she saw herself in the mirror for the first time immediately after her bilateral mastectomy—she was shocked at her reflection. Staring back at her was baldness, the bump on her skin from her implanted port, drains extending out from her sides, and fresh wounds where her breasts used to be. She felt like she was looking at a monster. Time passed. Her drains were removed. She finished her chemo. Her port came out. The wounds became scars. Her hair grew back. The reflection in the mirror changed. She saw scars that revealed how much trauma her physical self had endured. She realized her body didn't betray her. It had been fighting for her all along.

We begin shaping our body image at a very young age. There's a poignant TV commercial that shows a pre-teen girl looking at a virtually altered ad of a beautiful model, saying "I'm at risk of hating my body." Children compare themselves to see who is taller, smaller, bigger, skinnier... and the effects of not having what we perceive to be the perfect looks can last a lifetime. We are constantly bombarded with unrealistic expectations that very few can achieve.

How we feel about our bodies prior to diagnosis will certainly influence how we feel about it afterward. Because our breasts are part of what makes us women, breast cancer can exaggerate our pre-existing feelings and perceptions. We may feel less feminine, less attractive and less desirable; we may think we've lost the parts that define us as a woman.

We interviewed Ali Schaffer, a cancer survivor and licensed clinical social worker, who points out, "After being diagnosed with breast cancer, women tend to automatically disconnect from their bodies as a coping mechanism to help endure the invasive poking, prodding, and intruding into personal space. In this separation of the mind from the body, there is also a separation from feelings, from presence and awareness, in order to allow healthcare providers access to our bodies so that they can give care and provide treatment. While the disconnection often occurs automatically, the reconnection of mind, body and spirit does not—so we need to consciously and intentionally reconnect with our bodies as part of the recovery and healing process. A first step to intentionally reconnect with our bodies is to repeatedly tell our body that we're safe now, that it is okay to relax and that the threat has passed. Healing from cancer includes physical healing as well as emotional healing which includes the need to heal the relationship with our body. We don't ever have to love our scars, but maybe we can strive to accept our scars as a means to create peace in and with our bodies."

It helps to remember that our bodies are ever-changing, with or without cancer. We will go through menopause at some point in our lives, with all the physical and emotional side effects. It's okay to grieve the loss of the natural process, and to be angry that some of the side effects come too early, are heightened by sudden onset, and last longer. We don't all have the luxury of time to ease into this life transition, and that can leave us with a host of different feelings. And we are allowed to have those feelings, experience their depth and process them. This is a situation where the old saying that "time heals all wounds" is right on target most of the time. The more years that pass, the easier it is to forgive our bodies and accept the way we are now.

One JTW small group facilitator shares with her participants that she takes this a step further and actually thanks her body. She thanks her body for working on her behalf and showing up for her. She considers the positives and healing within herself as sort of a "love letter" from her body to herself. Expressing gratitude for everything she has been through and how far she has come.

Thanking your body reinforces the mind-body connection. It reminds you that your thoughts and emotions can influence your physical well-being. Gratitude toward your body after a rough journey of surgeries and treatments is a practice of self-love, healing and renewal. It can also aid in the need to intentionally reconnect with your body. Our bodies are incredibly resilient and deserve appreciation.

Karen had only been married for two years when she was diagnosed. She didn't have a pleasurable physical relationship with her first husband, and was surprised and delighted that intimacy with her new husband was "incredible." She felt extremely betrayed, hurt and bitter that she needed a bilateral mastectomy in her forties after just discovering a pleasure that had eluded her for many years. Pam, divorced and in her late fifties, said she felt guilty about not feeling a loss with her mastectomies. "I like my new breasts much better than my real ones!" she says. Rita, an active woman in her mid-thirties, still in the process of tissue expanders, reported that she really enjoyed being able to go braless and wear backless dresses—but also missed the "bounce."

All these reactions are perfectly normal and valid. As Ali Schaffer explains, "We must hold space for duality. We can feel both happy and sad about the changes. And we need to recognize that how we feel may be different from someone else, and that our feelings will likely change over time. We are all entitled to feel how we feel."

REFLECTIONS

1. How do you feel about your body now? How does that compare with your feelings prior to diagnosis?

2. What are some of the most significant changes that have occurred since diagnosis and treatment?

3. How have you been able to make peace with the "new you" and reconnect with your body?

SELF-CARE IS NOT A FOUR-LETTER WORD

Recovery and healing is a continuum. It changes over time, just like our bodies. While we are still reeling from having the veil of immortality suddenly yanked back, we are faced with a multitude of emotional and physical wounds. If ever there is a time for making self- care a priority, it is now.

As women, we are used to putting the needs of others before our own. We take care of our children, perhaps our aging parents; sometimes we have demanding jobs or other commitments that require our attention. During treatment we may be able to put some of these needs in the background. However, once we finish chemo and radiation and have that last surgery, we often find that others expect us to be back to our old selves, good as new. We may even have this same expectation, and we're surprised to find that we are quite different now.

"It's like a whole new body I'm in. I don't know how to deal with all these changes," says Elaine… and Jennifer and Susan and Sharon and Kellie and pretty much everyone else. Now is the time to reconnect with our bodies and get in touch with our emotions. It may be the first time in our lives that we've stopped long enough to actually care for ourselves in an intentional manner. Don't be surprised if you face resistance from others who are startled by these new actions. Stand firm, because as they tell us on airplanes: "Put your own oxygen mask on first." We must fill our own tanks to have what it takes to care for others.

We may not want to set health goals because we are afraid we may not be able to attain them. We don't want to set our expectations too high because "what if the cancer comes back?" There is a not knowing, an uncertainty that wasn't there before. It is important to prioritize ourselves and to create time and space to actively reconnect with our bodies and re/build the relationship with our body with curiosity and without judgment. Befriend and accept it. Do pleasurable things like getting a massage. If lymphedema is an issue, look for a massage therapist that has experience in this area. Find a recovery or support that is tailored to cancer survivors, or work with a personal trainer who is certified in working with those who have had cancer.

We interviewed Ali Schaffer, Clinical Social Work/Therapist, LCSW and received this advice: "If you exercised prior to your diagnosis, be prepared for the reality that you will need to start slowly and rebuild your strength and endurance. Remember that your body has been through a tremendous amount of stress and is still healing. Give yourself grace to push just hard enough to feel better and not overdo it. If you've had reconstruction, muscles and limbs may not feel or move the same way for a while. Take your time, adjust and move on.

Many of the women I have come in contact with over the years have never exercised, or it's been decades since they last worked out. Fueled with a desire to make a lifestyle change, they jump in with enthusiasm. This is great, but it's equally important to continue exercising long term. Not only does it help us connect with our bodies and make us feel better, a 2021 study published in the Irish Journal of Medical Science[34] found that the risk of recurrence was 63% lower in breast cancer survivors who exercised for two to five days a week compared to inactive participants. Learning mindfulness may also help with reconnecting and re-defining who we are now. Mindfulness is a psychological process of bringing one's attention to experiences occurring in the present moment. It has been shown to help ease fear and anxiety, as well as improving focus on achieving stated goals. There are therapists and others trained to lead mindfulness practice, but these aren't always necessary to learn how to live in the moment. Anything we do that brings our attention to what is going on in our mind and in our body in the moment helps us connect.

Restorative yoga, stretching or breath classes, tai chi, guided meditation and other such practices are all good places to start.

We will carry physical and perhaps emotional scars for the rest of our lives. We may be embarrassed or frightened by the physical limitations of our new body. Schaffer suggests that we invite curiosity about what else is going on in our life when something feels off, such as a new ache or pain. "Inviting curiosity shifts you away from feeling afraid of your body and powerless in your life, to feeling connected to your body, open to information and able to make decisions that feel good for you," she says.

We may worry that something is wrong with our body because it looks and feels different. That may cause us to apologize a lot for things we have no control over: "I'm sorry I don't have the energy to chair that committee. I'm sorry I can't carry the groceries in by myself now. I'm sorry I only wear baggy tee shirts." But we need to stop apologizing.

The purpose of self-care is not selfish or self-centered. It is a part of healing and recovery and renewal. The fact that you are reading this means that you are looking for these very things. We must keep body, mind, and spirit in balance as we continue on our journey to wholeness. We need to give ourselves permission to have autonomy and authority over who we are and who we want to be. Cancer is an opportunity for change, but not a mandate.

Going back to the story of the man at the Pool of Bethesda,[35] now is the time to honestly answer the question, "Do you want to be made well?" Only you can give yourself permission and power to make whatever changes you think are necessary (or not) to achieve "wellness" as you define it.

Self-care is also a way to celebrate life after overcoming signitficant challenges. It's a reminder that you deserve to live life fully.

REFLECTIONS

1. What does self-care mean to you?

2. Since your diagnosis how has your mindset toward self-care changed?

3. Share some things you do for yourself that bring you joy.

GIRL TALK

We've talked about the dangers of isolation and the importance of community. We've defined "community" as the relationships we have with others and with ourselves. Our intimate relationships fall into both categories.

Breast cancer treatment may affect intimate relationships in a myriad of ways. The aftermath of surgery can affect our body image, changing how we view ourselves in terms of being feminine and attractive. Physical pain cannot be ignored as a factor. The physical side effects of chemo and hormone blocking medications may include a loss of sexual desire and a change in response. The emotional side effects may include anxiety, depression, and unexplained crying jags. Obviously, none of these things are conducive to a good sexual relationship.

Intimacy can be difficult to talk about for some people, but having open and honest communication with your partner is vital. Generally speaking, men may find it more difficult to pinpoint and share their emotions—but it is no less important for them to do so. Try to find a quiet time to just talk and maybe even share the feelings chart we use in group. If you are open and vulnerable about your feelings, that may invite your partner to share theirs.

If your breasts were an important part of your intimate relationship, it is natural for both partners to grieve any losses associated with that. Remember that anger is a part of the grief process, as well as sadness. Perhaps working through these emotions together will bring you to a closer relationship, and facilitate acceptance for you both. Following chemo, a woman in her fifties shared in one of our JTW small groups that she and her husband chose to view her bilateral mastectomy as "a funeral for my boobs." At a funeral there is mourning over what's lost, but there is also a celebration of life. This JTW small group participant shared that she gave herself permission to mourn the loss of her breasts. She was grieving but also celebrating the life she got to keep. Now, five years later, she says, "Sometimes I still get angry and sad, but I've accepted the fact that my 'on' switch has been flipped to the 'off' position forever, and we just have to work a little harder to find a new one (on switch)."

Until you've shared your thoughts and feelings with one another, it's important not to jump to conclusions about your partner's reactions. You may discover your partner is afraid of hurting you and may wait for you to bring it up because of not wanting to push things too fast. Others may feel that everything is back to normal and "good to go" as soon as treatment is over, while physical intimacy is the very last thing on your mind. Instead of being angry, an explanation of where you are physically and emotionally may help your partner understand that things have changed.

There are things we might want to ask our medical care team about, but are either embarrassed or when we ask we find they don't have a good answer. The prevailing attitude in the oncology medical community is often "don't ask questions we don't have answers for." However, there are other medical resources available that can provide both answers and assistance. Look for women's health physical therapists or a clinic with licensed sexual health therapists.

Schaffer states, "A healthy intimate relationship may or may not involve sexual activity, but it's important that whatever way you and your partner choose to experience intimacy and affection works for both of you. Get in touch with your own feelings about your body and intimacy now. How have things changed? What exactly do you want from your partner? You need to create time and space to listen and learn about your own feelings and your own needs."

Intimacy is another area in which it can be helpful to have a support network of other survivors. Verbalizing changes, questions, concerns, needs, and desires with others in the same situation can help assure us that we aren't weird or hopelessly flawed. If you have trouble finding a way to communicate with your partner, saying things out loud with others may be a good rehearsal. Keep in mind that our intimate relationships change over time whether we have cancer or not. We grow older. Libido wanes for everyone. The important things are communication and continuing to share affection with those we are closest to, whether that's a hug, holding hands, or a roll in the hay.

REFLECTIONS

1. How has your view of your sexuality changed since your diagnosis?

2. How has the physical intimacy in your life changed since your diagnosis?

3. If you have a partner, what do you want them to know about your body, your feelings, your sexuality or intimacy?

MOVING THROUGH
LIFE'S LOSSES

*"I just know that old scars can break like fresh wounds
and your unspoken broken can start to rip you wide open
and maybe the essence of all the questions is:
how in the holy name of God
do you live with your one broken heart?"*

—ANN VOSCAMP

"So far, you've survived 100% of your worst days."

—UNKNOWN

DEFINITIONS AND STAGES OF GRIEF

Loss is defined as a situation or relationship no longer being the way that it once was. The effect of loss in our lives builds on itself if we do not process it completely.

What follows any loss is grief. Grief is a process that our minds and bodies go through to deal with loss. There are six stages of grief. These stages do not always happen in a linear order. We can experience them several times throughout the process.

Denial is a state of shock. Denial helps make survival in the beginning possible because it protects your mind and body from having to experience the full impact of the loss all at once.

Anger can extend to your friends, doctors, family, yourself, and God. Underneath anger is pain and a longing for understanding. Anger is strength during this time to give you temporary structure to nothingness of loss.

Bargaining focuses on "if only..." or "what if..." statements. You want to go back and fix it. Bargaining helps you admit any guilt that you have and leads to forgiveness.

Depression feels empty. You are in full surrender to the loss as your mind and body absorb it. This is completely natural, not something to "snap out of."

Sadness does not feel the same as depression. It is a more active state of feeling the full force of the loss. It hurts tremendously, but you are present and healing.

Acceptance is NOT about feeling 'ok' or doing 'all right'. Your heart is broken open to new beginnings. You accept the reality that you cannot change the past, or change your sadness. You begin to redefine who you are after the loss.

"Unresolved grief is almost always about things we wish we'd said or done differently, better, or more."[36] We can add that it is also that which we wish *were* better, different or more. It is so important for us to search our past and present for this unresolved grief, no matter how "unimportant" we think it is.

Our minds often put grief aside in order to keep moving. It's normal, but it doesn't mean the grief isn't important or that it's gone away. We grieve for many things: changes in seasons of life, including becoming a parent, death, divorce, finances, job loss/changes, death of a pet, moving, retirement, illness, empty-nest, loss of dreams/ideals/expectations, etc.

If we do not acknowledge the grief and work through it, we will stay stuck with the pain and not reach the stage of acceptance.

ALL GRIEF IS CONNECTED

There are undeniable losses that come with a breast cancer diagnosis. Some are obvious, like losing our hair or our breasts. Others, such as feeling a loss of femininity or trust, are more subtle. Some losses are hard to recognize, and others we simply dismiss, saying, "I should just be grateful to be alive."

With any loss there is an associated feeling of grief. Grief is the end of any normal pattern.

Grief is unresolved if you are still wishing for something to be different, better, or more.[37]

"I wish I had a different outcome with my mammogram."

"I wish the relationship with my husband had been better so it hadn't ended in divorce."

"I wish I'd spent more time with my mother when she was alive."

Grief does not mean just the end of something in our lives; it means the loss of everything that was tied to that normal pattern. So, even seemingly simple things like losing our normal routine can bring mourning. We need to acknowledge all the losses, small as well as large.

In her work with terminally ill patients more than 30 years ago, Psychiatrist Elisabeth Kubler-Ross observed that there are five stages of grief as one faces the end of life. Since that time, her theory has been applied to all types of loss and has been both praised and criticized.[38]

What we've come to learn is that most people will experience these stages of grief when faced with a significant loss, but it is not a defined, linear journey completed in a specific amount of time. We may bounce from one stage to another quickly, and then very slowly move on to another—or we may go backward before we go forward again. There is no right or wrong way to experience grief and there is no set timeline. We can even get stuck in any given stage.

Kubler-Ross identified the five stages of grief as denial, anger, bargaining, sadness and acceptance. Reall believes there is a sixth stage of grief. He observes that depression often comes before sadness. "When we're in depression we are not present; we are in a state of apathy," Reall explains. "Sadness means that we are present and feeling again."

It's helpful to know the stages of grief so we don't think we're weird or losing our marbles when we experience these feelings. We may want to just rush through and get to acceptance so we can put the cancer behind us and move on—but that's not how it works. Grief is resolved by completing all communication around the loss. You cannot grieve alone. We need others. There isn't a simple way out of grief but there is sitting with others. The process of telling our story helps us feel whole and is transformed. With a breast cancer diagnosis, community is mostly peer to peer, with those who have been through the same thing. Being able to feel like someone can truly relate to what you have gone through is a gift. It is a gift to be seen and heard in a safe space. Family and friends, as supportive as they may be, do not necessarily fill that gap.

Remember, too, that all grief is connected. It is cumulative. In her book, *Funeral for a Stranger*, Becca Stephens writes, "Sometimes we are grieving many things when one thing happens. I also think that if one ages well, grief grows deeper and deeper. What we grieve in the present connects us back to our losses."[39]

As we grieve our diagnosis and all it has brought with it, we may find ourselves unexpectedly grieving other losses in life. The reappearance of these losses may surprise us, but it is important and vital that we take the opportunity before us to grieve those unresolved events. If we do not, they will continue to linger, actually making the recovery from this experience harder and longer. As Reall says, "Living with loss begins in childhood—it begins simply with the loss of a favorite toy or the attention of our parents. Then we lose at sports or perhaps we lose a pet. We eventually lose our innocence...think of a glass slightly filled with emotional pain. Each time a new loss presents itself—and is not worked through—the glass gets fuller. Suffer enough losses and the cup runs over. This presents the image of major grief."

We need to take some time within this journey to begin distinguishing one loss from another to fully understand why we see and react to life in a certain way. As we talked about our individual paradigms in Day 9 and how we can change the meaning of our personal narrative, grieving our losses is a key factor. We cannot transform the story of our lives without coming to terms with the most important events that shaped our perspectives. Suffering and loss are likely the pivotal elements that have shaped us. It may not be what we want to hear, but it is true. None of us want to revisit those places of pain; we don't enjoy walking the stages of grief. But if anything is certain about being human, it is that we are like the Titanic—the more we try to avoid the pain, the more it will damage us. We must go back to move forward.

REFLECTIONS

1. Grief is the end of any normal pattern. How did your diagnosis affect the normal pattern of your life?

2. What do you wish were different, better, or more?

3. Name a loss from your diagnosis that you have not felt freedom to talk about?

WITH LOSS COMES CHANGE

The Grief Recovery Institute defines loss as "not getting what we want or expected."[40] As a human, we are a vessel that is empty at birth. As we grow through life, the vessel begins to fill with various experiences, including loss. In our culture, we typically aren't taught how to process the inevitable losses we face as we go through life. The unresolved emotions from disappointments, losses, and hurts weigh us down and distract us, making it difficult to hope and to be fully present. And make no mistake, we don't "move on" from grief—we move through it and we move forward.

There is a great deal of debate around the term "survivor" as it pertains to those who have lived through and beyond a cancer experience. The thought is that we have survived many things prior to this diagnosis, so cancer does not define us as survivors. In fact, you may prefer to be called a breast cancer "thriver," "overcomer," or "experiencer." But the truth is **we ALL survive** many types of losses all through our lives, up to and including breast cancer and we will continue to live through additional losses until the day we die.

Grief and love cannot exist without each other. They are two sides of the same coin. The greater the love, the deeper the grief. Grief will be part of every single one of us until the end of time because love is part of us.

We usually think of loss in physical terms, like losing a possession, the death of a loved one, a divorce, or some other major, easily identified event. But if we use the definition provided by the Grief Recovery Institute, that loss is "not getting what we want or expected,"[41] it becomes easier to understand that there are less tangible things, such as the loss of a dream, or the loss of faith and trust in one's body or in other people, the loss of innocence as we face mortality, or the natural timing of our life cycle. All of these are as valid a loss as any other.

The losses we experience in childhood, adolescence, and into adulthood are unique to each of us. The losses that come with breast cancer may also be individualized, but we do have many in common. The loss of femininity, libido, and the physical ability of our former selves seem to top the list, along with a loss of trust in our bodies, and a loss of identity—life has changed, so "who am I now?"—is a frequent question.

Each loss deserves its own mourning, whether that's a five-minute farewell or a five-year process of experiencing every stage of grief. Most, if not all, the breast cancer survivors I've walked alongside will tell you that the process of grieving the losses takes years. Even when we get to the point of acceptance of one loss or another, we may still grieve that particular part of ourselves that is gone.

I was forty-five years old when I was diagnosed with breast cancer. My children were six and nine years old. A corporate downsizing left me without a job in May of that year, and I was taking some time off to regroup and renew, planning to start my job search in January. Then, three weeks after my October birthday I felt the lump. In my heart I knew what it was, but I went immediately into denial.

While making the rounds of doctors appointments and all the associated testing in the following weeks, I zig-zagged from fierce denial to anger to bargaining. Sometimes it was one or the other, and sometimes it was all of it in one messy glop of fear. My thoughts went something like this: "I don't really feel anything. The doctors are wrong. They mixed up my biopsy results and I'm going to get a call any minute saying 'just kidding!'" (Of course, none of that actually happened, but denial can be a powerful distraction.)

I was also angrier than I'd ever been in my life. How dare God let this happen! I was a mother with two young children who needed me! I yelled at God at the top of my lungs while I mowed our back yard one afternoon, thinking that no one could hear me over the mower (my husband did, and wisely let me yell and cry it out alone). There was a physical release and some relief in all that emotional letting go, but it didn't change anything. I was still mad at God, at the environment, at fate, at Mother Nature, at the circumstance.

When I finished yelling, I started bargaining. "What is it you want from me, God? If you'll let this all be a big mistake, I'll do anything. I'll go to church every Sunday. I'll devote the rest of my life to whatever you want." If you'll do this, I'll do that—classic bargaining.

And all that was before I got my final biopsy results! After we knew exactly what we were dealing with and had a treatment plan, sadness entered the mix, too.

From then until now, almost 20 years later, I've experienced all the stages of grief for every loss associated with my diagnosis and treatment. And even though I've come to accept all the things, acceptance came at different times for each loss. There are times when I still get sad and mourn something lost along the way, and as I get older I find new losses to grieve. For me, the key has been accepting that I am not in control, but with God's help I can use all of the experience for good.

REFLECTIONS

1. Did you see yourself as a survivor before cancer? If so, due to what?

2. What feelings associated with grief make you uncomfortable?

LOSS AND DENIAL

Because most of us are not prepared or taught how to deal with loss as children, we find our own ways to cope. Many times that includes stuffing them away so we don't think about them, not realizing that each new loss is filling our life glass a little more. As we face the losses associated with our diagnosis, it's helpful to look back at our entire life and name what's already in our glass. Let's take a look at some common categories.

LOSS OF DREAMS

Childhood can be a magical time. Virtually your entire life is ahead of you. Anything and everything seems possible. As a little girl you may have dreamed of being a teacher, or maybe a pop singer or an Olympic gymnast when you grew up. Having dreams is a healthy thing. We need dreams and goals because they offer us a vision to live by. They add purpose and create a passionate connection with life. Dreams propel us forward into the future. But the loss of these dreams can bring us to a stalemate, causing us to become resentful and blame God. Scott Reall writes:

> "After the death of my dream (of becoming a professional athlete), I became resentful toward life, God, and ultimately

myself. I thought that perhaps if I had taken better care of myself or had been better prepared, I could have lived my dream. But it didn't happen, and I was furious with myself for failing. Eventually, I turned the anger inward and suffered from depression and isolation. I continued to chase crazy opportunities, trying to resurrect my dead dreams. When those didn't work out, I fell even deeper into despair. My discontent affected everything, and my marriage ended in divorce. Most of us are taught to pursue dreams, but few of us learn how to cope with their loss. Yet most of us will hold tight to dreams that don't come true. Even though we pursue and strive for them, we often fall short of seeing the dream fulfilled. How we respond to this loss will have huge implications on the quality of our lives. It's essential that we learn how to move on when life doesn't turn out the way we had planned. My inability to understand the loss of my dream cost me almost twenty years of my life. I faced depression, addictions, and divorce—all because I was ill-prepared for dealing with the loss of my hopes and dreams. I never processed the losses. I never discussed them with a trusted friend. I struggled in silence. We will all experience dreams that do not come true. It's important to grieve these losses so that God can bring about new dreams. When I got married, I had blissful dreams that I would be happy forever. But I wasn't. Marriage didn't empty the half-full glass of grief that I brought into the marriage. I now realize I had grandiose ideas about marriage. I thought it would be the catalyst to take away my pain, but this myth only set me up for more loss."[42]

In the book, *From Hurt to Hope*, author Farrar Moore shares, "I was not taught how to process loss. Consequently, I was oblivious to a need to teach that to my children. Losing my doll, watching my quarter roll into a street drain, watching my dad drive away without me, ripping my new coat, my best friend moving away, the death of my grandma, being very sick, not making the team, striking out, dropping the pass, losing an election, feeling left out or ignored, being misunderstood or ridiculed, the divorce of my parents, abuse, injury, rejection—our list can go on and on. The loss just kept happening."[43]

LOSS OF INNOCENCE

When we are children, we are like pristine lakes. Throughout life, ships run aground and spill oil and sludge throughout the lake, eventually killing the fish and birds. The black oil has contaminated the once beautiful water, rocks, and shores. Contamination may come in the form of physical, spiritual, or emotional abuse. Usually there's some tragic or troubling event, such as a divorce, that wounds the childlike spirit. For some, these wounds never heal. Trauma doesn't have to come from a single moment. It can result from a parent who tells you repeatedly that you'll never amount to anything. It can come from the fear of living in an unstable home. Perhaps you were touched inappropriately, or you were expected to provide emotional support for an adult.

Maybe you were simply never told that you were loved and valued. Or maybe you had to make a significant move and were unable to settle into your new environment. All of these are tragic childhood losses. The loss of innocence can be one of the more difficult losses to grieve, because we frequently cover up this sort of loss.

LOSS OF A LOVED ONE

We usually think in terms of death when we think about the loss of a loved one, but there are other ways we might lose the ones we love. Losing a parent or spouse to Alzheimer's disease is heartbreaking, as is the loss associated with various types of mental illness. Sometimes we lose a close friend because of relocation or perhaps a betrayal. The loss of a loved one may be the greatest loss of all. It is a pain that never completely fades, but it can heal. We can find peace in the midst of our loss.

LOSS OF PLACE

We experience loss of place in many ways. The change from high school to college, from college to leaving home. Losing the familiarity of our childhood, with all the associated memories, can be difficult. Some experience this loss frequently, if their parents or guardian moved homes multiple times, if they had to attend different schools and constantly make new friends, or if they were in foster care. We may decide to move to a new city, sell the house our children grew up in or transition to a community or assisted living situation. There can be loss of place at retirement, when we are no longer part of the workforce. There are many ways in which we can find ourselves in an unfamiliar territory, physically or emotionally, where the landscape of our lives is no longer recognizable, and we grieve the loss of what was.

LOSS OF IDENTITY/ROLE

We transition through many roles in our lives, but often overlook the grief associated with this change. There is always something new coming around the corner at every age and season. Moving from childhood to adolescence and then to adult life. Being a single person to being a married person, a married person to single. We may spend years recognizing and reconciling our sexual or gender identity which can be a painful process of acceptance and understanding. There is a certain grief over becoming a mother, even when we are told that should be the happiest moment of our lives. Yet it still marks a tremendous change in our lives forever. Then when children leave home, we transition again to a life without them. We may consider ourselves a contributing part of the workforce but then choose to leave for family or health. Or leave our roles at home to pursue a career. Every time we turn a corner and redefine our role in life, there comes with it some grief at leaving the past behind and moving on. But if we recognize that it is normal to be sad over these times, it makes it easier to move through.

LOSS OF LOVE

The dreams and expectations we have often involve sharing our lives with another person. Our first real heartbreak from a romantic relationship can be a devastating rejection to move past.

Sometimes we look but never find that special someone to share life with, or perhaps we find them but the relationship doesn't work. And when a partnership or marriage ends, the loss of the dream traumatizes everyone involved—not just the couple. It's a pain that's hard to accept. What we want, what we expect, what we hope to have in life is often very different from what happens. As the venerable Harry Emerson Fosdick wrote, "Very few persons have a chance to live their lives on the basis of their first choice. We all have to live upon the basis of our second and third choices."[44] This is hard for most of us to accept. We aren't willing to live with second or even third choices. In America, that's considered failure. But we need to come to grips with this reality and understand that no loss is too great to overcome. For many people, marital expectations do not materialize.

There is an idealistic hope of what marriage is going to be, and it doesn't match up to reality. The reality is that marriage involves two imperfect, flawed people attempting to connect. It can be messy and difficult. It can disappoint at times, and it takes work, communication, commitment, and intimacy. We inevitably find that no person, no relationship has the power to give us the significance and purpose that can only come from God. The responsibility for making our relationships successful lies in the work we do individually with God because when we're growing spiritually, we have so much more to offer a partner.

LOSS OF SUCCESS

When we try something new and fail to accomplish our goal, we experience a loss. The greater our desire for something, the greater the risk that we will be hurt if we don't get it. Sometimes people desire something so much that they will not risk the hurt of failure and just won't try at all. It is inevitable that we are going to fail at some things we attempt in life, and with failure comes a sense of loss. We need to work through losses because if we close our hearts due to painful failures, we stop living the adventure of life. Life is sometimes like a game of dodgeball. You can continue to dodge situations that have the potential for loss, or you can stand there and try to catch the ball. Let's look at the life of a person who had significant losses in his life but never gave up: Abraham Lincoln.

- He failed in business at age 21.
- He was defeated in a legislative race at age 22.
- He failed again in business at age 24.
- He experienced the death of his sweetheart at age 26.
- He had a nervous breakdown at age 27.
- He lost a congressional race at age 34.
- He lost another congressional race at age 36.
- He lost a senatorial race at age 45.
- He failed in an effort to become Vice President at age 47.
- He lost another senatorial race at age 47.
- He was elected President of the United States at age 52.

Obviously, Lincoln worked through his losses and continued to move forward, accepting new possibilities and new challenges. He persevered. Had he not, our country might have been forever changed for the worse. In the face of such challenges, many of us probably would have retreated and given up. But Lincoln's faith in God was a driving force. He believed in the abilities God gave him, no matter what the circumstances told him. And so he persevered.

Like Lincoln, we can develop resiliency and move on to greater possibilities. We can look back and realize that life hasn't been a complete failure. It's as Henri Nouwen once wrote: "We find new courage to let new things happen, things over which we have no control. And it is here that we find courage to face our human boundaries and hurts, whether our physical appearance, our being excluded by others, our memories of hurt or abuse, our oppression at the hands of another."[45]

REFLECTIONS

1. Name one significant loss you experienced in childhood. How did you feel about it then and how do you feel about it now?

2. Is there one: loss of innocence, loss of place, loss of love, loss of identity/role, loss of success, loss of a loved one that has affected your life more than another?

3. When thinking about all the losses throughout all your life, where does breast cancer fall in terms of significance?

ACKNOWLEDGING THE ANGER ASSOCIATED WITH LOSS

The moment we begin to deal with our anger over our losses is when we've moved on from denial. Once we can no longer deny the loss, reality hits, and we experience anger. We ask ourselves—or we ask God—"Why did this have to happen to me? This just isn't fair." When our wishes, dreams, and plans are thwarted, we might feel that fate or God has somehow robbed us.

Most of us have certain expectations about how our life should be. When these expectations aren't met, disappointment, resentment, and anger may follow. Often our expectations coincide with a sense of entitlement. We think God should bless us and give us what we want. This is a dangerous line of thought. When we start feeling entitled, it's natural to become angry when those expectations are not met. We need someone to blame. Sometimes we blame God or others, and sometimes we blame ourselves.

Anger itself is not a negative feeling. Often we are taught to ignore or stuff down our anger. But healthy anger can propel us forward, like when we decide we are no longer going to put up with bad relationships or a toxic job or some injustice in our community. Anger must be present for any change to happen or anyone to challenge the status quo. However, if we ignore anger and refuse to process it, it turns into resentment which leads to unforgiveness. We might hate a spouse for divorcing us, hold onto ill will towards an employer who passes us over, or be angry with a friend or family member who suddenly disappeared after our diagnosis. Some of us even feel angry with loved ones who die. And at the heart of most resentment is anger toward God. We blame God for not giving us the life we wanted and expected.

Author and actress Carrie Fisher wrote "resentment is like drinking poison and waiting for the other person to die."[46] When we harbor resentment, we stay stuck sometimes for decades—unable or unwilling to move on. Resentment is kept alive by remembering all the wrongs done to us. The animosity and bitterness we hold inside is a simmering anger that we keep returning to like a clean pig returns to the mud. With chronic resentment, we often turn our anger inward, and it can develop into depression.

Regret is another way we can experience anger, and sometimes resentment. As humans, we are notorious for punishing ourselves with regret. What if I had married someone else? What if I had finished college? What if I would have been in a different place at a different time? We can scrutinize situations and decisions for years, but it won't change the past. Instead, it empowers us to remain a victim instead of focusing on our present and future.

The "could have/should have/if only" syndrome can pop up after a cancer diagnosis just like any other painful loss. If only I'd eaten better/ exercised more/not gained weight/not lived in a polluted city/not been stressed… the list goes on. Anger can be a healthy, natural emotion. But when anger becomes a chronic resentment or bitterness, we stay stuck in this phase of the grieving process. Until we can move to the next stage, we cannot conquer our grief and begin to grow. As we've said, life is about loss. We cannot go back or change things that have happened. Instead, we can look to the future with a new vision. God always has a better plan than we can comprehend for each of us. God can pick up the leftovers of a broken plan and turn them into something beautiful. Instead of resenting God's change of plans, go with it! When you can't see God's hand, trust God's heart.

KELLIE'S STORY

When I was diagnosed, I was angrier than I've ever been in my life! My husband had passed away unexpectedly a year earlier. My mother had Alzheimer's, and we'd just made the difficult decision to put her in a care facility. My father was also having health issues and not coping well with my mother's situation. My oldest was ready to leave for college and my youngest was in the midst of middle school angst. I just thought, "Really, God? Seriously? After everything else, now I get breast cancer?"

This was not how I expected my life to turn out. My plan was to marry my prince and live happily ever after. We would grow old together, spoil our grandkids, travel. My mother was supposed to be there for me whenever I needed her. This just wasn't fair!

I was bitter and resentful for years. Then one day my sister told me I'd become a crabby old woman, even though I was only 53. I was hurt, angry, and shocked. She was supposed to be my rock now... how dare she criticize me like that! I held on to that resentment for several more years, becoming more and more depressed, just going through the motions of life.

Looking back, I see now that I felt entitled to the life I'd imagined. I was angry that my dreams were dashed, that life wasn't playing out like I'd always thought it would. I was angry at myself, blaming my breast cancer on all my past lifestyle habits and bitterly wishing I'd made different choices. I was angry at God for letting all these horrible things happen. I just couldn't believe that a loving God would let me suffer so much.

I finally decided to change my circumstances. I had heard about the health benefits of social connections and shared life experiences. I was ready to do what it took to make myself healthier. I joined a support group for widows, and made friends with another breast cancer survivor. As we talked each week in group, I began to see my circumstances in a new light. I called my sister and apologized, and we resumed our formerly close, loving relationship. I learned to sit down and take time to work through things that had been taking up valuable space in my head and my heart. I owed it to myself to do the work. And even if I couldn't see changes on the outside of me, I wanted to make a difference on the inside. Once I let go of the anger and resentment, it seemed as if I was suddenly seeing the sunshine again after a long, dark winter.

REFLECTIONS

1. If you could ask God why something specific has happened in your life, what event or situation would you ask about?

2. In your anger over loss, who are you angry with? God, yourself, someone else, or all the above? Explain.

3. Considering you only have control over yourself, what do you need to do to get rid of a resentment in your life?

BARGAINING

The third stage of the grieving process is bargaining. It is often an outgrowth of anger, as the realization that life is changing begins to sink in. In an effort to avoid the pain in grief and loss, we bargain with God, others, even ourselves. Our goal is to make a deal so that we can go around—instead of going through—the pain or suffering that comes with a loss.

A big part of this bargaining game often involves God. If God gives me what I want, I promise to give God something back. God doesn't want to be a form of escape from our problems. God is more concerned with our hearts than our circumstances. We have to come to grips with the fact that God may choose not to change our circumstances, but will use circumstances to change us. We must own a genuine sense of responsibility and approach God with an 'I will allow You to change me' attitude. This is not a conditional if it's an authentic response. We can't manipulate God. God does not respond to ifs."

One of the problems with loss is that we often can't see how anything good could possibly come from the experience. There tends to be a darkness around us that conceals any ray of light. And yet, the Bible reminds us in Romans 8:28 that the good is out there, even when we can't see it: "We know that in everything God works for the good of those who love him."

The misunderstanding of God leads to the following logic: "If I make these certain moves then God will provide what I wish for."

Then, when things don't go as planned, we feel cheated. We wonder if we did something wrong or that God didn't live up to his end of the bargain. Just as we bargain with God or others, sometimes we also bargain with ourselves. We tell ourselves that we are going to do this or that, or we will never make the same mistake again. It's much the same as when we try to manipulate or bargain our way out of dealing with reality. This may give us some great goals to strive for, but we must also be realistic and not expect the changes to happen overnight.

Sometimes in the midst of our grief, we feel like we have a brick wall in front of us and regret at our backs. When this happens, we just need to have patience. If we feel like we can't move forward, it's okay to just stand still! There's no way to go around grief—we must just go through it.

Consider the possibility that God may want to provide comfort and meaning in the face of adversity, offering an opportunity to trust and surrender to a higher power. Try putting anger and fear aside for a moment. Look for solace in the belief that our challenges in life serve a greater purpose or are part of a life that ultimately helps us grow emotionally and spiritually.

Thanks to scripture we know what we're supposed to do. There is reward that comes from the intrinsic motivation to trust and follow God. If we try to define what He is doing along the way—we may be disappointed with the outcome. Our life's journey is known to Him and is revealed to us as we live. God's "deal" for us is better. As we go through the pain and the trials of life, know that God is making a way and that you will come out on the other side stronger for the experience.

REFLECTIONS

1. When have you bargained with God in the hope of getting a
   different outcome?

2. How do you accept the fact that we cannot and will not know all
   the reasons why we have to go through suffering and difficult
   situations?

DEPRESSION AND SADNESS

Sadness and depression are also normal stages of the grieving process. After we experience denial, anger, and bargaining, we may become depressed and then sad—all our emotional efforts so far have not changed our circumstance and we are still facing the pain of loss. When things don't turn out the way we'd hoped, or when we face divorce, death, loss of employment, an illness, or some other loss, we are susceptible to falling into depression. When we don't address the anger we experience after a loss, sometimes we become numb to the pain. We lose our drive to get up and get out of bed. Life becomes gray. We don't feel anything—we don't want to feel anything. Things that used to bring joy and excitement no longer stir our hearts or our sensibilities.

Sadness is a natural response to loss. Minirth and Meier have a great description of sadness in their book, *Love Is A Choice*: "Sadness is the healthy means to relieving pain and loss."[47] Sadness is ordinary. Sadness is the appropriate response to sad events. Best of all, sadness is not endless.

Unlike chronic depression, repetition and suppressed anger, sadness comes, is recognized, and goes. This is when you settle down for a good, old-fashioned cry. You may want to cry alone, but at times you might find it very helpful to do your crying on a sympathetic shoulder. Give yourself time at this stage, don't look for any quick fixes. There's a lot of wisdom in the old saying, "A good cry cleanses the soul." Visualize your tears washing away your pain.

There is a transition between depression and sadness that is a healthy transition. The process begins when we experience depression over our losses. We become angry, turn it inward, and feel life is not worth living. The transition comes when we move from that state into sadness, where life becomes worth living again, and we are able and willing to feel. There is sadness still, and we miss that which has been lost, that which was so meaningful. But we stop being angry and depressed.

Dr. Chip Dodd refers to sadness this way: "Sadness is the feeling that speaks to how much we value what is missed, what is gone, and what is lost. It also speaks of how deeply you value what you love, what you have, and what you live... One of the gifts of sadness is that it is the first step of healing from loss. Sadness is fundamental to a full life because it opens up the door to healing."[48]

He goes on to explain that sadness is proportional—the more you value something the more it is going to hurt. Some of us are sad when we lose our hair, but we realize that it will eventually grow back. The point is that the depth of sadness we experience with each loss is unique to each of us, depending on the things we value most.

There may not be a clear-cut, proven method for moving out of depression into sadness, but one of the most helpful things you can do is to communicate with someone. Fortunately, many oncology centers now employ mental health professionals to serve in this role. This situational depression is very different from clinical depression. Often, talking with a mental health professional or even a small group of survivors with a trained facilitator can help move us from depression to sadness. Clinical depression, on the other hand, requires medical intervention.

Sadness is a turning point in the grieving process. Each of us will deal with the stages of this process differently. For some, sadness may not be intense, but they might feel that way for longer. Others might experience brief, but tremendous, sadness. As you begin to float through bouts of sadness, you are nearing the final stage of grief, which is acceptance. When you finally move toward acceptance, you might still experience sadness. But it's an emotion you are willing to feel and perhaps even embrace. Once you can move through these stages and understand their benefits, they will move you toward healing, where you can focus on the finish line.

If you can approach the sadness stage with honesty about the things you are missing, you will be able to expedite the grieving process. With certain losses, you may even be able to experience memories with the sweetness and joy that they originally brought. You can sit back and remember the pleasure, and let the sadness of your heart honor those times.

We'll talk more about acceptance later, but at this point it's important to understand that acceptance does not mean that our grief comes to an end. With the types of loss we may experience with breast cancer, we might always feel some sadness. Acceptance means that we are no longer fighting for control; we can also find joy in spite of the pain and sadness of that particular loss. As Connor Gwin writes, "There is no magic ladder out of grief and we will not magically ascend above our suffering. Instead, God descends into our pain and redeems it through the cross of Christ."[49]

REFLECTIONS

1. Since your diagnosis have you experienced depression? If so, how are you dealing with it?

2. How do others in your life allow you to be sad?

3. How would it look if you gave yourself permission to be sad?

PROCESSING OUR LOSSES

*"God gave us memory so that
we might have roses in December."*

—J. M. BARRIE

"We need never be afraid of our tears."

—CHARLES DICKENS

*"What is stronger than the human heart
which shatters over and over and still lives."*

—RUPI KAUR

*"Grief, I say, come in. Sit down.
I have tea. There is honey.
This will take as long as it takes."*

—THIS HALLOWED WILDERNESS

PROCESSING OUR LOSSES

Give your grief the space it needs to exist. Feel the not-so-good feelings. Feelings are messengers with a story behind each one. A story worth sharing. The more we acknowledge our feelings, the grief and sadness, the greater the opportunity for healing.

One of the most effective ways to process our losses is to spend time writing them down. The time we give our brains to contemplate the types, frequency, and significance of our losses, the more healing occurs. This week is dedicated to doing this important work through our Loss History Graph and our Loss Letter from The National Grief Institute.

LOSS HISTORY GRAPH

- Start at the date of your first conscious memory of loss
- Draw a line across the page
- Above the line, write down the date and age of the loss
- Below the line, write what the loss was.
- Make the length of the line according to the significance of the loss. A huge loss will be a long line. A lesser significant loss will be a shorter line.

- You may want to use a pencil for the vertical lines because as you proceed through your graph you may decide you want to make adjustments as to the length of the loss line.

After you are done, reflect on your life losses. Do they show a theme or pattern?

Did they start early in life or later? Are they consistent throughout?

Have you included losses like: Loss of trust? Loss of safety? Loss of innocence? What was/is the most significant loss in your life?

How has that loss affected your life overall?

Did you discover losses that you had forgotten or diminished?

Was there a season of your life where you had many losses together? How has that affected you? What grief in your life is still unprocessed?

What is your biggest realization from doing this exercise?

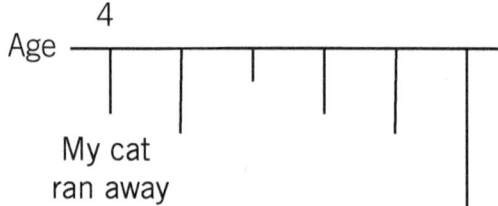

James & Friedman, *The Grief Recovery Handbook* (HarperCollins, New York 1998)

LOSS LETTER

Identify a relationship in your life that has held great significance for you in terms of its influence on your life and any unresolved grief it represents. Write a letter expressing everything this relationship has meant to you; how it has challenged you; how it has affected you and all the feelings that you have around that. It may be that you aren't writing to a person, but loss through an event or situation or time period in your life where you have felt trauma or grief. For instance, one survivor wrote her loss letter to the sadness she felt moving away from her hometown of 65 years across the country to another state.

One survivor wrote her letter to cancer. One survivor wrote a letter to fear. Your options are wide open. You won't be giving this letter to the person you are writing to. **This is meant to be an exercise for you to express completely your thoughts and feelings to help resolve unexpressed grief and to move toward acceptance.** This letter is for you and your own healing... no one else.

Below are four real examples of loss letters shared during JTW small groups written to something other than another individual. (Used with permission.)

EXAMPLE ONE

Dear Cancer,

I hate you. You have taken more from me than I can express (including my Mom when I was only 15 years old).

But let's get personal. You showed up at MY house, at my door, and barged in. You were an uninvited intruder. We were helpless to throw you out once you entered. Instead, we were forced to have a front row seat to your intimate destruction. Yes, ultimately you were kicked out of our house (for now), but you didn't leave until you had stolen sacred things from me. When you robbed, you bypassed the jewelry, the china, the electronics. Instead, you looked hungrily at what I thought couldn't be stolen... my BODY... my security.... my identity..... my very being.

But (and this is a beautiful but), I am slowly learning about your value. You have been the thorn in my flesh that drove me to Christ.[50] I have learned true, complete surrender and obedience to the Lord in the face of barbaric evil. I now know myself at a level I could have never known any other way. I stared directly into the eyes of sorrow—held the hand of fear—taken a turn on the dance floor with the thought of my own mortality, and emerged on the other side. By my own strength? Certainly not! It is the Lord Himself who has carried me (and still does). He gently threaded his fingers into mine and gently led me away from the edge.

Cancer, I will continue to learn from our unfortunate time together— my journey isn't over and I will be dealing with the fallout of your invasion for the rest of my life. This, however, I DO know: What you meant for my harm, the Lord intended for my GOOD.[51]

EXAMPLE TWO

Dear Kellie,

I heard your voice from within scream "me, it's me" when I was asked to write a letter to my greatest loss. You lost yourself. You were born into a family that didn't understand your emotions, empathetic nature and desire to please everyone around you. You wanted to believe that everyone was good and genuine, but the truth is they were selfish and inconsiderate. Survival came in the form of a brick wall around your emotions. You had to keep the hurt and disappointment hidden. It was just too painful to face alone.

Enter your cancer diagnosis. The brick wall that was in place hid your grief, fear and sadness from everyone around you, including yourself. You had to be strong for everyone else, you can't show any weakness. YOUR FEELINGS ARE LAST. You convince them that having no hair was very convenient, when the truth was you felt so ugly. When no one offered to drive you to treatments, you simply said "it's fine I can drive myself" because you didn't want to ask and appear weak. When the truth was sitting in those treatment chairs with an IV full of poison was the loneliest you had and will ever feel. Crying in the shower the morning of your double mastectomy so they wouldn't see. Only to arrive at the hospital with a smiling face and telling everyone that having new boobs at 30 was going to be great. Then swallowing the lump in your throat when you saw yourself in the mirror because you felt like a freak. All of this was to protect THEIR emotions at the cost of your own. The suppressing of your own emotions was becoming more detrimental to your health than the cancer itself. You were dying but not from the cancer. The only way to survive at this point was to become a new and "improved" Kellie.

You did find a strength somewhere along the way that you are grateful for today. But you are tired. You want to be heard and appreciated for the real of you, not the one forced by circumstances. You can tear down the wall and fight your way back. You can still be strong and stand up for yourself. You can find balance in the compassion for others and your own self-care. You can be ok with letting go of relationships that do not nourish your soul. You can forgive those that knowingly or unknowingly hurt you. That forgiveness is for you, not them. FORGIVE YOURSELF. Most of all know it is OK to love yourself. That does not mean you are selfish.

You can be the best of both versions of yourself. The old and new can merge into the beautiful being that God intended for you to be. HE gave you life for a reason. HE makes no mistakes, and HE has a purpose for you.

EXAMPLE THREE

Dear West Coast Life,

As I sit down to write this letter, waves of nostalgia wash over me just like the crashing waves I used to watch from your beautiful shores. When I came to you as a young 11 year old girl—I had no idea the sort of life that I would be building with you for the next 56 years. You provided home, surroundings, and activity.

Living on the west coast wasn't just about the geography—it was about embracing a lifestyle that resonated with me at a deeper level. But, beyond the physical mountains and ocean—you gave me life, community, family, and friends.

Leaving you behind meant leaving behind a piece of myself. Leaving behind a huge piece of my identity. And leaving something IS losing something.

More specifically—what I've loss by leaving are/is:
- *The busy years of family building*
- *The love and success of volunteering*
- *The opportunity for leadership roles*
- *The fellowship of a church family*
- *The daily interaction and exercise with close friends*

I left this life on purpose with the joy of knowing that my new home would provide the close physical family I had missed having nearby for fifteen plus years. I just didn't realize what a difficult transition it would be.

Until we meet again, West Coast, know that you will always hold a piece of my soul.

EXAMPLE FOUR

Loss Letter - Life 2.0

At 54, the path traveled has been a rugged one. One that has transgressed peaks and valleys. One that has led me to believe I am on my journey alone.

In childhood, I felt like a parent tending to the needs of my family. My father worked two jobs was mostly absent. My mother was codependent. My older brother was jealous and aggressive. I grew up believing I had to "earn" love.

As a child, I didn't have the connections of living in a town with other families and being part of a larger tribe. As a teen, in an act to make my family notice me, I attempted suicide.

As a young adult, my relationships were with people who took advantage of my weaknesses and vulnerabilities. I failed to listen to my inner voice and leave the relationships that were not going in the right direction.

I married and became a mother of two beautiful girls. I found complete joy in nurturing and loving them. As a professional, I chose a company whose values aligned with my own. At 49, I had the realization that I needed to build a stronger vessel, my body, that could voyage another 50 years. (Fittest @50)

As I came into my diagnosis, there was the realization that I needed to uncover my authenticity and enter the arena of my vulnerability. Opening the door to my authenticity, I asked my husband to love me, to give me the security of really feeling his love for me, to help me feel that I mattered to him. And it turned into the demise of my marriage. My greatest need, then and now, was just to feel loved. What I got instead was a rise in intimate partner abuse. He drove me away, and I learned that my youngest child was also being abused.

I lost my security, safety, money, house, neighbors, friends, love, fitness, joy, health, my ovaries, and of course, my breast. And what I gained was fear, shame, hurt, loneliness, and PTSD. Now I move forward. Forward to live my purpose. Starting again with new friends and someday, a new love to explore the next 50 years.

ACCEPTANCE AND SEEING
THE GIFTS

*"When we deny the story, it defines us.
When we own the story,
we can write a brave new beginning."*

—BRENÉ BROWN

*"Healing may not be so much about getting better,
as about letting go of everything that isn't you—
all of the expectations, all of the beliefs—
and becoming who you are."*

—DR. RACHEL NAOMI REMEN

NEW BEGINNINGS

Acceptance is the final stage of grief. It comes when we make peace with what has happened. It's not a switch that suddenly floods our soul with light, but is instead a gradual process. Acceptance comes in stages. Much like forgiveness, it's important to understand what acceptance is and what it is not. Acceptance does not mean that I'm happy about what happened or that I'll never again feel the emotional sting of my experience. Although my heart has been broken, acceptance means I am now open to new beginnings. I accept the reality of a past I cannot change and now see that I have an opportunity to redefine who I am going forward. It's important to remember that the stages of grief are cyclical, it's not a linear process. Don't give your emotions a timeline. All living things go through cycles, it is the nature of being.

There are so many losses associated with breast cancer we couldn't possibly make peace with all of them at the same time. Acceptance of some losses comes easier and more quickly than others. And like all the stages of grief, acceptance is not an endpoint. We may arrive there and then find ourselves angry or sad all over again. The passage of time can also play a significant role in reaching a stage of acceptance.

The central step in the process of moving to acceptance and coming to peace is forgiveness. The way we move through the grief stage of depression is by learning to accept what has happened and forgive those who played a role. Forgiving those who've hurt us, forgiving ourselves, and even forgiving God for the hurt and losses in our lives, frees us from depression and grief. It dissolves the anger toward the person or thing that has hurt us.

Christ tells us that forgiveness is for us, not for the person (or thing) that has hurt us. If we forgive, we can live by the fruit of the Spirit[52]: love, joy, peace, patience, kindness, goodness, faithfulness, gentleness and self-control. Resentment is the cause of many chronic struggles for those who withhold forgiveness. Whether we're angry at a person or a situation, we must ultimately accept the reality of what is and move toward forgiveness. Of course we're going to feel anger at the injustice and unfairness of certain events in our lives, but holding on to pain is like drinking poison. The only antidote for resentment is forgiveness. When we forgive, we let go of the past. This cracks open a space for the future, allowing us to be in the present.

We talked about forgiving our bodies and ourselves in the context of being kind to ourselves. More than 10 years after being diagnosed in her forties, Jennifer remembers when she began the path of acceptance that finally brought peace.

"I was so very angry," she says. "I felt betrayed—by my body, by life, by God. I hated the mounds on my chest where my breasts had been. Several years after I finished treatment I was in the shower one morning, soaping up and feeling the familiar rage as I quickly slid my hands across my chest. For some reason, that morning I decided that my anger and hatred weren't doing me any good and might be poisoning me on a cellular level. I made a conscious decision to finally welcome my new 'girls' into the family. That act of forgiveness was the first of many small steps toward acceptance of what I'd gone through."

One way to measure where you are in the process of acceptance is to examine the fruit of the Spirit in your life. Are you experiencing these on a daily basis? What is your life producing? When we harbor bitterness in our hearts we aren't able to experience the fruit of the Spirit. When we don't forgive, when we don't accept the losses in our lives, we are not living—we are merely existing.

When bad things happen, it's very common to question God. Why do bad things happen to good people? Much has been written on this subject and yet we still struggle to understand how a good and loving God could permit such pain. Why would He allow a mother to get cancer and risk leaving her children without her love and guidance? Without getting into a full theological discussion on human suffering and pain, the short answer is that we don't know. But open-ended hope allows us to trust Him when we don't understand.

This is where faith becomes more than just a "feel good" philosophy for life. This is where it gets hard. Faith is believing that God is right in the middle of it with us. It's okay to admit that we don't understand how and why this life works. That doubt makes us human. Scott Reall says:

> "A pastor once said that the problem with death by suicide by young people is that they haven't lived long enough to experience how things change over time—that losses in our lives eventually give way to new beginnings. Recognizing the new beginnings is a significant step in helping us move forward. When we forgive others, our circumstances, and ourselves, we are able to see that new beginnings are possible. When we realize we are powerless and stop trying to control everything, instead, turning that over to God, we set ourselves in position to accept the meaning God will make from all the mistakes, pain and suffering we've experienced to bring us to this point."

REFLECTIONS

1. What are some things you have accepted related to your cancer experience?

2. What do you still have trouble accepting related to your cancer experience?

3. Now that you've completed the loss graph you have acknowledged several deep losses throughout your life. What are some things you've accepted related to those significant losses?

RECLAIM. REFRESH. RESPECT.

Acceptance is essential in the grieving process. If we never move into this stage, if we stay behind in our grief, it will keep us from living life to the fullest. Living in grief keeps us from the people and things that are in the present. If we're trapped in the past, we'll miss out on everyone and everything that is still moving forward.

In order to find completeness in our grief and get to this place of acceptance, we must complete all communication around the loss(es). The things inside you that need to be grieved simply do not go away in isolation. Even though it's often hard and painful, that's why we complete the Loss Chart and share them in our group.

Katie summed it up when she said, "Now I feel so much freer, like a weight has been lifted off. There may always be reminders of my cancer, but that's just my reality now. I can accept that and move on with my life."

There may be parts of our life that we really like and want to keep, and there may be other things that we want to change. We may now feel a stronger sense of urgency to make some changes because we are all too well aware that if we wait until tomorrow to change, tomorrow may not come. But desiring to make a change and taking the action necessary to actually make that change are two different things.

Why is it so hard? Dr. Patrick Carnes says one answer is that change is about reclaiming integrity.[53] It's about respecting ourselves enough to do the hard work of change. Sure, it's easier to be a couch potato than hit the gym three days a week. But laziness leads to a lack of self-respect, and it's hard to change if we don't respect ourselves enough to do so. Recovering from an inactive lifestyle means that we will have to reclaim integrity, and reclaiming integrity is about self-respect. And remember that self-respect starts with how we judge ourselves. We then put that energy out into the universe—and that is how the rest of the world starts to see us as well. Having self-respect begins when we accept ourselves as God sees us. When we accept ourselves,we understand that we may have to work on our faults. Hating ourselves ties one arm behind our back. Charles Reynold Brown, dean of Yale Divinity School, once said,

> "Everyone is born into the world with a certain unrealized capacity. Let him accept his hand as it was dealt to him, and play the game, without wasting his time bemoaning the fact that his cards are not all aces and faces. Accept yourself for what you are, and for what, by the grace of God, you may yet become and play the game."

The Bible says that all of us should set aside everything that hinders and run the race that is set before us. No one gets to choose his or her race. We don't get the opportunity to choose between being perfect and being imperfect. All of us are imperfect. The key is to "set aside" the things that are keeping us inactive in the process of change, such as laziness, self-defeating addictions, poor boundaries, and listening to the inner critic that tells us that we will never change or be better than we are right now. The ability to set healthy boundaries requires that we respect ourselves enough to do so. You are worth it!

Having self-respect also means being ourselves in every situation. Charles Reynolds Brown wrote, "Some people are hypocrites because they try to appear much better than they really are. Other people are hypocrites because, for some reason, they are afraid to allow that which is true and fine in them to be revealed."

Self-respect includes living a life of humility, where we understand and accept our limitations. This means we realize we aren't Superwoman.

We can't change our lives without God's help– not just in one area, but in all parts of our life.

There's a difference between humility and self-deprecation, which means belittling or undervaluing oneself. True humility is also acknowledging the things we're good at. It goes back to being true to ourselves, accepting imperfections and using the talents that God gave us. It's about embracing who we are—all of our strengths and weaknesses.

Gaining self-respect is a result of setting goals and achieving them. We feel good about ourselves when we achieve goals. There is great satisfaction in setting SMART goals.[54] SMART goals consist of goals that are:

Specific
Measurable
Attainable
Realistic
Time-sensitive

Putting in the work and meeting our goals makes us feel empowered. That's one of many reasons exercise is so central to any breast cancer program. Some participants start the program weakened from cancer treatment and months of inactivity. Each time they increase the amount of weight they use, or go faster or longer, it helps return the self-confidence that is often lost in the long road from diagnosis to recovery. Self-confidence is a building block toward self-respect. It takes consistency, persistence and perseverance, but when we accept ourselves with humility and truly become who God made us to be, we become something different and something better.

REFLECTIONS

1. What does having integrity mean to you?

2. Are you able to recognize and acknowledge the things you're good at? Do you "own" those talents or do you dismiss them when someone comments or compliments you? Name three things you acknowledge you are good at.

3. What goals have you set for yourself during this time of recovery? Which have you achieved and which are you still working on?

STEP OUT OF THE LIFEBOAT

In the New Testament of the Bible, Matthew tells us a story about taking risks. One evening, Jesus sent his disciples across the lake and a storm came up. The men were afraid, but then they saw Jesus walking toward them on the water, saying, "Have courage! It is I. Do not be afraid." In a situation like this, most of us would have been relieved and invited Jesus into the boat. But Peter, the adventurous one, wanted to walk on the water, too. He called to Jesus, "Lord if it is really you, then command me to come to you on the water." Jesus said, "Come." So, Peter stepped out.[55]

The riskiest step of any new venture is always the first step. It's the bravest, too. Take Peter, for example. Our logic and understanding of the scientific rules of this world tell us that we can't walk on water because a human weighs more than water. It is a scientific fact that a human will sink. But sometimes we have to defy our logic and understanding. So why don't we take that first risky step to change? Often, it's because we don't want to let go of the familiar. Change breaks the rules; something different happens. This fear is what keeps us in the boat, where we are comfortable.

To change anything in our lives or to accept that life is going to look different than before, risk will be involved. But think about it— every day we're involved in activities of risk: driving a car, flying in an airplane, swimming in the ocean, using a power tool. If we attempted to stay away from these things, we'd be stuck on the couch in our house and never get out or do anything. But each day we push out into a world of the unknown, where anything can happen.

We discount the courage we already have shown by choosing to be in a relationship, to love another person, sacrifice for another, forgive, let go.

Think about one thing you're afraid of. Anna was terrified of almost everything in a theme park, especially heights and things that move very fast. In between finishing chemo and her next surgery, she and her husband decided to take a short vacation with their two children to a water park. Her kids begged her to go down the "world's tallest water slide" with them. Her first thought was to send them with their dad while she watched, but she was already feeling the sting of the many activities she'd missed with them during chemo. She thought to herself, "If I can survive two surgeries and six months of chemo, surely I can survive going down this water slide!" Down she went.

For Anna, that was stepping out of the boat. It's a simple, physical analogy of one thought process that can be used to take that first risky step toward change. Anna had to trust that God would be with her, no matter what.

Whatever the changes we contemplate, we first have to step out of our comfort zone and take a risk. Maybe you want to change your lifestyle, eliminating negative habits and adopting healthier behaviors. Maybe you want to stop apologizing. Perhaps you want to change your inner narrative. Change for you might be getting out of a toxic relationship. It might mean changing jobs, retiring or going back to work. The point is that some change is subtle and some is more visible, but it's in our power to direct any changes we desire. Much like the grieving timeline is different for every individual, so is gaining the courage to take a risk. Anna decided to step out of her comfort zone early on. You may need more time to gain the courage to take a risk. In Soni's culture it wasn't easy or common practice to burden your family with a scary medical diagnosis. It was only after being in community of the JTW small group that she gained the courage to share with her parents that she had battled breast cancer two years earlier. With this newfound courage she was also able to leave a job she was miserable in. Soni told her group she felt like a weight had been lifted off her and there was a visible countenance change in her face. Soni's courage had a snowball effect. She redefined her life in those moments by taking brave steps to become who she truly wanted to be.

REFLECTIONS

1. Think about a time when you took a risk? What happened?

2. What is the "boat" that you need to step out of in order to change?

3. What is a risk you might be avoiding that actually might improve your life?

STAYING THE COURSE

As we come to accept our circumstances, we realize that we aren't the same as we were before our diagnosis. Whether our diagnosis was a stage 0 or stage 4 a new life is upon us. We can't alter that fact; we can only choose how we respond. As we read yesterday, that response may include taking a risk and making changes that we desire.

If this is the case, we start by accepting the risk, then taking the first step—but we can't stop there. H. Jackson Brown, Jr. reminds us that "In the confrontation between the stream and the rock, the stream always wins—not through strength but by perseverance."[56] Making progress in our plan of change requires that we show up, do our part, and trust God with the results. If we focus on progress and not perfection, it gives us the determination to stay the course.

Progress is a path of small transformations that take place each day. It's a process. Mistakes and setbacks will inevitably happen. But when we start again we get better. This is how we transform. Change doesn't happen with one large step, but with multiple baby steps. One of the best ways to keep going toward our goal is to be aware of our progress over time. It will happen if we just keep showing up and working on it.

Marcy was an avid recreational tennis player before she was diagnosed with breast cancer. She enjoyed not only the physical challenges, but also the social aspect of playing the game. When her world felt like it was turned upside down for a full year filled with multiple surgeries, chemo, and medication that made her body feel years older than her actual age, she felt she would never be able to step on the court again. Outside of fearing she would not be able to have the stamina to play, she was also scared..... scared of moving her "new body." All sorts of images and thoughts came to mind. Was she more susceptible to injury now that her muscles had been moved and stretched out over implants? What about the 17 lymph nodes the surgeon took? Would her arm swell? And what about the fact that she was still getting used to even the balance of her new body.... what if she fell? Or if she got hit by the ball in the chest? All the concerns fit right into a "paradigm of worry and fear" she was carrying around after cancer. But on the other side of all the surgeries and treatments—Marcy decided to lace up her tennis shoes and get back in the game. God had held her hand through the storms of the past year—she could do this! She knew how much she enjoyed the activity and camaraderie with friends and cancer wasn't going to win if she had the ability to get up and move. Maybe she wouldn't be in the running for Wimbledon, but she knew she needed to get back out there and start over because of what she gained from playing. So with a whole lot of self-compassion she gave herself permission to fail and began to work on surrounding herself with friends who were patient with her slow, baby-steps progress. The first time she walked out on the court after a year of not even picking up a racquet—she was so nervous. She barely held the racquet for more than 15 minutes—but considered it a huge success and felt like she had conquered Mt. Everest. Sometimes just showing up is half the battle. Within the days, weeks and months that followed—she spent more time moving around and learning to trust herself, giving herself grace to take things slow and learning (again) how to play the game she loved so much.

In Day 5 we talked about intrinsic versus extrinsic motivation in the context of hope. As we move closer to acceptance it may be easier to see that meaning will come from this experience, and that may provide the intrinsic or internal motivation to continue on our path of change. When we're intrinsically motivated, it's not about making anyone happy or trying to avoid a consequence. It's an internal desire to work together with God from a perspective of "I want to be different." We focus on who we are becoming and commit to being in it for the long haul.

As we begin to accept the beginning of a new life after cancer, looking at changes we may want to make, it can help to look at life before cancer. Did it compliment who we are, or did it distract us from our purpose? Sometimes reassessing and renaming our situation can revolutionize us.

What we all hope for at the end of the day is to emerge from our struggles a better person. Sometimes we hold tight to old ways, even if they are detrimental. Accepting changes happens when we focus on the solution to a problem more than on staying where it's safe. We always have choices. Always. Fate is not our master.

Cancer does not define us. I don't think I would ever say that I'm glad I had cancer, but when I look in the rear view mirror, I can see many good things that came from it. Once I worked my way through all the stages of grief to acceptance, it allowed me the freedom to explore changes that have made my life much better. I was able to let go of some habits and thought processes that weren't healthy, and I learned new ways that have allowed me to be a happier, more productive person who is healthier physically, emotionally and spiritually. I decided to be my own best friend. You can do this, too!

REFLECTIONS

1. Name three specific things that you want to be different about your life going forward.

2. How can you make these things happen?

3. In what ways do you want to be:
   Authentic

Healthier

Peaceful

Creative

Connected

CHANGING THE LENS

If we've examined our life "BC" (before cancer) and determined that we need to toss some old ways of thinking, negative behaviors, or find renewal, we need to have a vision of what we want our life to look like "AC"(after cancer). Remember the story about Michelangelo chipping away at the block of stone, working to set free the angel inside? That's what you've been doing these last eight weeks, and now it's time for the angel to fly.

As we begin to shape our vision for our life AC, it may help to reflect on the benefits of our diagnosis. It's empowering to look back and analyze all we've been through; we can identify a power and strength we may not have known we were capable of. We accept that reality isn't always comfortable, but denying it doesn't make it less real.

Our challenges have pushed us to look for something more meaningful. We obviously were ready for positive changes—otherwise you wouldn't be here now! We've put the effort into naming the losses we've experienced in life and that has taken immense courage. Our adversities in life become more daunting when we don't acknowledge them. But once named there is a power shift inside us. The hardships in this world give us the opportunity for greater appreciation of the incredible joys in life. There are no flowers without rain. There is no rainbow without a storm. There are no mountaintops without valleys. Life's tragedies **can** soften us. They **can** make us view the world in a more empathetic, loving and kind way. IF we let them.

Vickie confides that she can now "cut through the 'fluff' in life" and discern what's really important. "I no longer sweat the details," she says, "and that includes worrying about what other people might think. I don't want to waste my time playing games."

Maria says she's more aware of her boundaries and no longer feels guilty for enforcing them. "I've learned that I need to take care of my own mental and physical health, and sometimes that means saying 'no.' If it isn't something that brings me joy, I let it go." This meant making a change from full-time employment to working part-time so she could spend more time with her son. "When I was always stressed with working all the time, we didn't do fun things like bake cookies together. That brings joy to both of us. Work can wait."

Ashley, a JTW small group facilitator, told her group that she prayed to God her suffering would not be wasted. She asked Him to give her a place to invest it. She did not want her cancer journey to be in vain.

Kathy shares that she has a whole new perspective on life. "I'm not the perfectionist I once was. I've learned to forgive myself when things aren't perfect, and now I don't procrastinate so much. I've begun to live life more intentionally, making my own choices that aren't dictated by someone else's priorities."

Felicia says that she used her cancer experience to invest in others. "Because of my own losses, now I feel others' loss more deeply. Once I got to the stage of acceptance, it was no longer all about me—I feel this desire, this need, to pay it forward and give back to others. I know firsthand the importance of showing up. If I can make the world a better place; if I can help another person; then my experience will not have been in vain. It gives a purpose to what I went through."

Life is full of a lot of noise. Facing death reframes how we look at our lives—we realize just how precious life is. For at least a moment during our journey we pause and are forced to take it in. Struggles sometimes bring clarity we need to become the most aware of the fragility of life. It's in this space where we have a chance to make changes. Set a path that can be more fulfilling for growth to honor this precious one life God has given us on earth.

Not discrediting the pain but remember the quote, "You have survived 100% of your worst days." Pat yourself on the back! And just like every time before—you will find yourself on the other side. Isaiah 43:18-19 (NLT) says:

> "But forget all that—it is nothing compared to what I am going to do. For I am about to do something new. See, I have already begun! Do you not see it? I will make a pathway through the wilderness. I will create rivers in the dry wasteland."

What do you see for your future? It's been said we don't believe what we see, we see what we believe. What do you want? Believe it. See it. Claim it. Go for it. The future is yours and you're not alone. God is your waymaker.

REFLECTIONS

1. What are some gifts of your diagnosis?

2. How do you view life differently now?

3. How do you see your life a year from now?

LIVING THE DASH

We know we've reached acceptance when we come to terms with the fact that whatever it is that we've lost is gone forever. A season of life is over. Our hearts are broken, but now they are broken open to new things—open to new beginnings.

We accept that we can't change the past so we begin to move on and don't get stuck in regrets. We have a vision. Some of the best growth in life is because of this experience. You can be better, rather than bitter. We have a keen understanding that we get only one shot at life, so we resolve to live it to the fullest.

If we look at a tombstone, we see the year the deceased was born and the year he/she died. In between those dates is a dash—representing all the years between birth and death. A beautifully written poem by Linda Ellis titled *Living the Dash* speaks to the reader about living life to the fullest, about the value of the "dash"—which is life.

"Living in the dash" is about embracing the present moment and making the most of the time we have between birth and death as symbolized on the tombstone. It's a reminder that life is not just about the milestones or achievements—but more so, about the journey itself. There are many moments that make up our dash—each representing an opportunity to create memories, forge relationships, and pursue passions. What is holding you back?

"Living the dash" encourages us to focus on what truly matters in life: love, kindness and personal growth. It reminds us to cherish the people around us and strive for meaningful experiences. As we mentioned in Day 14, it's living authentically. It's about setting our own parameters. We get to choose. Ultimately "living the dash" is about leaving a legacy of love, compassion and positivity. It's about leaving our corner of the world a better place than we found it.

There is a quote by Peter Strople, a relationship-based business strategist, that states it even more clearly, "Legacy is not leaving something for people. It's leaving something *in* people."

It's possible to lose the urgency of the dash. We've all heard the phrase "in life there are no dress rehearsals." This is our only journey, and we must believe the path up hills and down into valleys is worth the walk. The itsy bitsy spider kept climbing up the waterspout because it believed the sun would shine again, no matter how many times the rain came down and washed it out. We have to believe the dash is worth living.

However, the dash requires effort. It takes a lot of energy to climb the highest peaks and dig out of the deep valleys. Most accomplishments come through tremendous perseverance. We all face the noonday demon: the drudgery of our jobs, our drab existence, the meager pay. The Bible says that life is like running a race. There's the start, the middle, the end. The final lap is the hardest. The middle is where we spend the bulk of life—the dash is where we truly live.

None of us know when the dash will end. There is no better time for change than now. Mark Twain once said, "Never put off until tomorrow what you can do the day after tomorrow." We humans tend to say, "I'm going to do it—starting tomorrow!" But it seldom happens.

Those of us who have stared death in the face have the gift of feeling the urgency of living our dash fully. It is the door of opportunity to become the person we've always longed to be. We have been in a state of transition, some for months and some even for a year or longer. We know that we are not the same. The choice then becomes: will we spend our dash trying to go back to where we were, or will we use our dash to create a legacy of the person we want to be. How do you want to spend your time? Do you want to embark on new frontiers? Do you want to improve upon the path that you're already on and be a better version of yourself?

God has a vision for us, a dream for our lives. Our lives have purpose. Will we sit back and let our spirits die within us while we miss the most incredible gift– the gift of the dash? With God's help we can overcome anything, and we can move forward and achieve great things.

Sunflowers represent healing, hope, longevity and lasting happiness. Their internal circadian rhythm causes them to follow the sun. The warmth of the sun feeds and strengthens them. They naturally turn east at night in anticipation of the sun rising, moving throughout the day to face west for the evening sun set. Like the sunflowers on the cover of this book, when darkness falls upon us, we can choose to turn our faces toward the Son for warmth, strength and growth.

Abraham Lincoln said "In the end, it's not the years in your life that count. It's the life in your years." Let's craft the life we want, the dash we are happy with and the legacy we want to leave in others.

"She is clothed with strength and dignity,
and she laughs without fear of the future."

—PROVERBS 31:25 (NLT)

REFLECTIONS

1. What legacy do you want to leave in your dash? In other words, what would you like to be remembered for?

2. Now is the time for change. What new beginning are you open to?

CREATING YOUR VISION PLAN

"The secret of change is to focus all of your energy, not on fighting the old, but on building the new."

—SOCRATES

WHAT WE'VE LEARNED SO FAR

We've covered a lot in the last eight weeks, so before we begin working on our plan to design our "new normal" and make it what we envision, it might be helpful to have a quick review. You may want to go back and read your answers to the reflection questions for each week before you begin writing your vision plan.

We've discussed the difference between hope and wishes; that true hope is not tied to circumstances. We may not be able to control our circumstances, but we can choose how we will respond and react.

Sometimes those responses and reactions are based on what the inner critic has played on repeat all through our lives. We can train, rather than try, to change that narrative. We are striving for progress, not perfection, as we take baby steps toward change.

We also identified the stages of grief and how moving through them is a process that is not at all linear. Even after we've gotten to acceptance we may go back and visit anger or sadness; the difference is that we don't stay there as long. We know that grief is cumulative. All the unresolved losses of our lives build upon one another until we complete all communication around each one. That's what we did when we shared our loss graphs. We cannot heal in isolation. Once we let go of our old baggage, we can stop living in the past and enjoy the freedom to look ahead.

But like the story about the man at the Pool of Bethesda, we must look inside and determine if we truly want to be made well. Are we ready to accept and embrace the changes that will bring? If so, valuing ourselves is one key to change. Self-respect begins when we accept ourselves the way God sees us; when we can be ourselves in every situation; when we live a life of humility; and when we set goals and work toward them. To have the new life we want, we must have vision, and to reach our new vision we must take risks. We must "step out of the boat" and walk toward God. Vision is not goals or accomplishments—vision is the type of person we want to be. Vision defines what we will become. It creates great passion, and passion comes from purpose. Richard Leider writes, "Purpose is the conscious choice of what, where, and how to make a positive contribution to our world. It is the theme, quality, or passion we choose to center our lives around."[57] We may need to ponder how we can make a positive contribution to ourselves, recognizing that we are part of "our world." And last, to achieve vision, we must persevere. It's easy to give up when we don't see instant results, but we remember that we're taking baby steps—doing the cha-cha rather than taking one step forward and two steps back—and while we may not be perfect, we are making progress!

WRITING YOUR VISION PLAN

Now you're ready to write out your vision plan, including the three pillars of wholeness: spirit, mind, and body. We will share these with the group. Here are the steps:

MY VISION FOR MY NEW LIFE

Write a brief assessment/history of your life up to your diagnosis and treatment. Describe where you are in your life journey. This may include your name, age, health status, challenges you've overcome in the past, things you know to be true about yourself, current feelings about your circumstance, your relationships, recurring fears, etc.

Write your goals for your spirit, mind and body.

Examples:
Spirit: Reconnect with God and develop a daily relationship.

Mind: Reduce stress levels and begin to feel a sense of relaxation. Begin to feel a sense of joy, peace, and purpose for my life.

Body: Mindfully eat nutritious foods instead of grabbing the easiest snack. Exercise at least 150 minutes per week.

Write the steps that you will take to meet those goals.

Examples:
Spirit: Read a devotion, Bible, etc. every morning, Mind: teach my family to use the Feelings Chart.[58]

Body: Put unhealthy snacks on the top shelf of the pantry and take group fitness classes 3 times a week.

List the people who will support you in these goals.
In addition to family and friends, think about your small group,
personal trainers, dieticians, health care team, church group, etc.

**What would your life look like if you accomplish
these goals?**

**What might get in your way on the way to these
goals? How can you begin to plan for overcoming
those obstacles?**

Write a few long-term goals...your "bucket list."

Write a personal daily prayer or your "mantra" or your favorite quotes for inspiration.

NOTES

1   Henri Nouwen, *Seeds of Hope* (Bantam,1990)

2   C.S. Lewis, *The Problem of Pain* (United Kingdom: The Centenary Press, 1940)

3   Scott Reall, *Journey to Freedom* (Self-Published, 2023)

4   John 5:6 NKJV

5   Psalm 139:14

6   Scott Reall, *Journey to Freedom*, (Self-Published, 2023) 5.

7   Gerald G. May, *Addiction and Grace* (San Francisco: HarperSanFrancisco, 1991)

8   Robert Brault, *Round Up The Usual Subjects* (CreateSpace, 2014) 140.

9   James O. Prochaska, John C. Norcross, and Carlo C. DiClimente, *Changing for Good* (New York: Avon Books, 1995)

10 Victor Frankel, *Man's Search for Meaning* (Beacon Press, 1946)

11 Charles Franklin, *Create the Life You Need!: Find Passion and Success Now With This Manual of Simple Practices* (Terra Nova Books, 2012)

12 Thom Rutledge, *Embracing Fear and Finding the Courage to Live Your Life* (San Francisco: Harper San Francisco, 2002), 1.

13 Irvin D. Yalom, *Existential Psychotherapy* (Basic Books, 1980)

14 Susan Jeffers, PhD, *Feel the Fear and Do It Anyway* (Ballantine, 1988)

15 Romans 8:38 NLT

16 Lewis B. Smedes, *How Can It Be All Right* (Pocket Books, 1986) 187.

17 Matthew 5: 1-2 NIV

18 Chip Dodd, *Voice of the Heart* (Franklin, TN: Providence House Publishers, 2001) 35.

19 Chip Dodd, *Voice of the Heart* (Franklin, TN: Providence House Publishers, 2001), 137.

20 Chip Dodd, *Voice of the Heart* (Franklin, TN: Providence House Publishers, 2001), 35.

21 Scott Reall, *Journey to Freedom*, (Self Published, 2023), 38.

22 Chip Dodd, *Voice of the Heart* (Franklin, TN: Providence House Publishers, 2001)

23 Matthew 22:12-13

24 Chip Dodd, *Voice of the Heart* (Franklin, TN: Providence House Publishers, 2001), 8.

25 Chip Dodd, *Voice of the Heart* (Franklin, TN: Providence House Publishers, 2001)

26 Sarah Young, Jesus Calling (Thomas Nelson, 2004)

27 Richard Rohr, "Grace Is Key" *Center for Action and Contemplation,* February 1, 2016. https://cac.org/daily-meditations/grace-is-key-2016-02-01/

28 Carl G. Jung, *Man and His Symbols* (Doubleday, 1964)

29 Gerald G. May, *Addiction and Grace* (San Francisco: HarperSanFrancisco, 1991)

30 Richard Rohr, *Immortal Diamond: The Search for Our True Self* (Jossey-Bass, 2013)

31 Julia Cameron, *The Artist's Way* (New York: Jeremy Tarcher/Putnam, 1992)

32   Brené Brown, "The Midlife Unraveling", *Brené Brown,* May 24, 2018. https://brenebrown.com/articles/2018/05/24/the-midlife-unraveling/

33   Henry Cloud and John Townsend, *God Will Make a Way* (Nashville: Integrity Publishers, 2002), 153.

34   Nadiye Akdeniz, Muhammet Ali Kaplan, Mehmet Küçüköner, Zuhat Urakçı, Şahin Laçin, Emre Hüsnü Ceylan, Abdurrahman Işıkdoğan, "The Effect Of Exercise On Disease-Free Survival And Overall Survival In Patients With Breast Cancer" *PubMed*, Epub Oct 4, 2021. https://pubmed.ncbi.nlm.nih.gov/34606055/

35   John 5

36   James & Friedman, *The Grief Recovery Handbook* (HarperCollins, New York 1998)

37   James & Friedman, *The Grief Recovery Handbook* (HarperCollins, New York 1998)

38   Elisabeth Kübler-Ross, *On Death and Dying* (Macmillan, 1969)

39   Becca Stephens, *Funeral for a Stranger* (Abingdon Press, 2009)

40   John W. James, Russell Friedman, *The Grief Recovery Handbook* (Harper Collins, 1998)

41   John W. James, Russell Friedman, *The Grief Recovery Handbook* (Harper Collins, 1998)

42   Scott Reall, Journey to Freedom (Self Published, 2023)

43   Farrar Moore, *From Hurt to Hope* (Crowned Image Publishing, 2016)

44   Harry Emerson Fosdick, *Riverside Sermons* (New York: Harper and Brothers, 1958), 54.

45   Henri Nouwen, *Seeds of Hope: A Henri Nouwen Reader* (New York: Image Books, 1997)

46   Carrie Fisher, *Wishful Drinking* (Simon and Schuster 2012)

47   Robert Hemfelt, Minirth-Meier Series, *Love Is A Choice* (Thomas Nelson, 1989)

48   Chip Dodd, *Voice of the Heart* (Franklin, TN: Providence House Publishers, 2001)

49   Connor Gwin, "The Ubiquity of Grief (and How I Tried to Climb the Ladder)" *Mockingbird* June 8, 2016. https://mbird.com/theology/the-ubiquity-of-grief-and-how-i-tried-to-climb-the-ladder/

50   2 Corinthians 12:7-8 NIV

51   Genesis 50:20

52   Galatians 5:22-23

53   Dr. Patrick Carnes, *A Gentle Path through the Twelve Steps* (Center City, Minn.: Hazeldon, 1993), 1.

54   Doran, G.T. "There's a SMART Way to Write Management's Goals and Objectives. Journal of Management Review, 70, 35-36", *Temple University*, 1981. https://community.mis.temple.edu/mis0855002fall2015/files/2015/10/S.M.A.R.T-Way-Management-Review.pdf

55   Matthew 14:22-33

56   H. Jackson Brown, Jr., *Life's Little Instruction Book* (Rutledge Hill Press, 2000) 11.

57   Richard Leider, *The Power of Purpose: Creating Meaning in Your Life and Work* (San Francisco: Berrett-Koehler Publishers, Inc., 1997), 26.

58   Chip Dodd, *Voice of the Heart* (Franklin, TN: Providence House Publishers, 2001), 137.

CONTINUE YOUR JOURNEY

As you continue in pursuit of the person God created
you to be, may you find these resources helpful, as well.

JOURNEY TO FREEDOM is a 36-day contemplative journey to help you understand your personal story and inner life more fully and compassionately. It will guide you through the stages needed for internal transformation, and allow you to find your own path toward emotional, spiritual and physical well-being.

JOURNEY OF TRANSFORMATION: CREATING THE LIFE YOU'VE ALWAYS WANTED is a 36-day contemplative journey to help you understand your personal story and inner life more fully and compassionately. It will guide you through the stages needed for internal transformation, and allow you to find your own path toward emotional, spiritual and physical well-being.

JOURNEY TO LIVING WITH COURAGE helps you address daily and persistent fears that impair your fullness of life. Fear is an inevitable part of being human, and it is a healthy part of your full emotional life when it functions to help you prepare, use discernment and keep you safe. But what happens when occasional fear turns to underlying worry and anxiety, robbing you of joy and peace? This book encourages you to acknowledge, expose and explore those persistent fears and the life experiences that inform them so that you can find a sense of security, practice courage, and move forward with hope.

JOURNEY TO A NEW BEGINNING AFTER LOSS helps heal the unacknowledged losses and disappointments in your life. From birth, you experience deeply profound losses that shape your story and circumstances. Your life is impacted by grief through intangible losses like unrealized dreams, unmet expectations, loss of innocence, trust, belonging, and self-worth. Or through tangible losses like finances, health, work, relationships, community, or death. Have you allowed yourself to truly grieve these losses? Do you feel that current losses bring up painful reminders of previous losses? Does lingering regret or resentment hold you back from a full life?

JOURNEY TO A LIFE OF SIGNIFICANCE helps you heal from the wounding of low self-worth. You may believe the lie that you will never be good enough, and so you strive to earn the love you long for and need. This book encourages honest self-reflection and movement toward acknowledging the inherent goodness and uniqueness God has placed in you. Uncover and examine the deeply rooted internal messages that hold you back from believing you are worthy, beloved or acceptable. Build a platform of self-worth to stand on that will positively impact all areas of your life.

PODCAST: Join us each week on the podcast *Searching Inward*

WEBSITE: restoresmallgroups.org

YOUTUBE CHANNEL: *A Moment of Hope* – @AMomentofHope-nu5dx